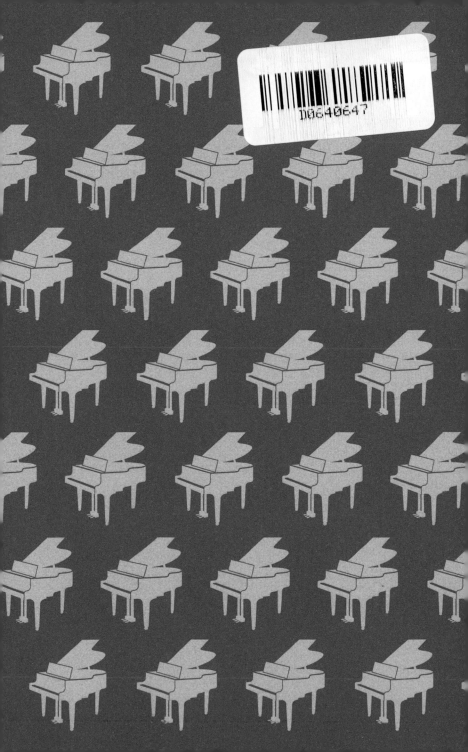

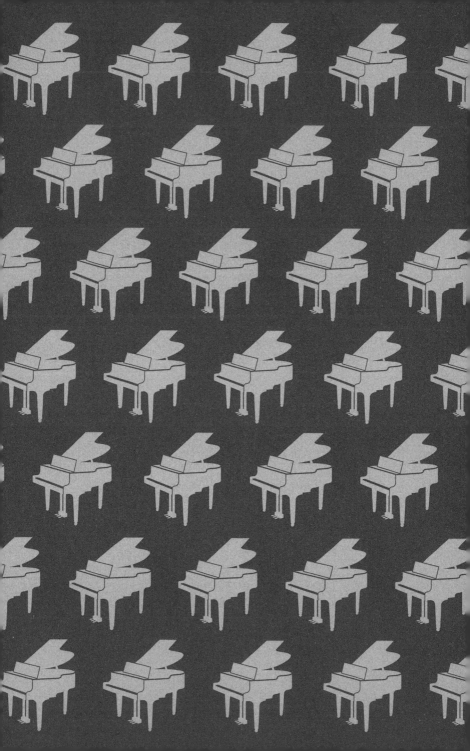

FOR THE LOVE OF
CLASSICAL
MUSIC

FOR THE LOVE OF CLASSICAL MUSIC

Summersdale Publishers Ltd
46 West Street
Chichester
West Sussex
PO19 1RP
UK

www.summersdale.com

Printed and bound in the Czech Republic

ISBN: 978-1-84953-732-2

Substantial discounts on bulk quantities of Summersdale books are available to corporations, professional associations and other organisations. For details contact Nicky Douglas by telephone: +44 (0) 1243 756902, fax: +44 (0) 1243 786300 or email: nicky@summersdale.com.

FOR THE LOVE OF
CLASSICAL
MUSIC

A COMPANION

CAROLINE HIGH

summersdale

For my daughter, Louisa
To my friend, Bronwen
And remembering Kevin

CONTENTS

INTRODUCTION

" *There are a million things in music
I know nothing about. I just want
to narrow down that figure.* "
ANDRÉ PREVIN

WHAT IS CLASSICAL MUSIC?

'Classical music' is an expression which depicts a certain type of musical style, but what sets it apart from many other genres is that it is written down. When a classical composer writes a piece of music, they do so with the exact notes they want each instrument or soloist to perform, and use specific musical directions, such as pitch, tempo and volume, to indicate how to do it. In brief, then, classical music is an amalgamation of order, design, content and form.

There's also a period in music – from the mid 1700s to the early 1800s – which is described as the classical period. Confused? Don't be, because a look at the way musical styles, including the classical period, have developed over the centuries will help you understand how the pieces we listen to today have evolved.

For the purposes of this book, the musical periods featured are medieval, Renaissance, baroque, classical, Romantic and late Romantic, the twentieth century and modern. And with all these musical periods, change didn't happen overnight – there were composers who bridged the end of one period and the beginning of another, and there were old-school composers who baulked outright at the new musical ideas that were evolving, so the dates are used as a general guide.

MUSIC THROUGH THE AGES: PART ONE

MEDIEVAL PERIOD: c.500–1400

It was an age of startling musical contrasts, sacred and secular; of troubadours and minstrels; of songs of chivalry and courtly love; of dances; of being entertained at dinner with lutes, bagpipes and recorders. But the medieval period was also a great age of church music, and you'll often hear musical terms such as plainsong, neumes, monophonic and polyphonic music, and modes, to describe this genre.

Plainsong, or Gregorian chant (attributed to Saint Gregory the Great, c.540–604), was a flowing, single melody chant without accompaniment. These early monophonic (one voice) chants were passed on orally, as the earliest medieval music had no notation system. But as single melody music gave way to the more complex polyphonic music (two or more voices singing in harmony), the need for a system of writing music down became apparent, and so the predecessor of our modern musical notation was born, in the shape of neumes – small square symbols which were written over the text to act as reminders of the tunes that were already known, but without note value or rhythm.

This period also saw the introduction of church modes, sequences of eight notes that helped classify the chants – a simple version of the scales we know today.

Notably, a lot of the attributes of medieval music formed the basis of some of the musical forms that we use today, and it was much the same with instruments, some of which have evolved to become recognised members of the classical orchestra.

Recommended listening

The songs of Saint Godric (*c.*1065–1170) demonstrate a monophonic melody line very well, as do the Gregorian chants 'Dies Irae' ('Day of Wrath') and 'De Profundis' ('From the Depths'). The Gregorian chant 'Deum Verum' ('True God') is a good example of polyphonic music, as it introduces voices singing in harmony (that is, combining different pitches of note).

And for accompaniment

We've all heard of the harp, the bagpipe, the lute and the recorder. But are you familiar with the bladder pipe, the shawm, the rebec, the citole, the cittern or the oud? Here are just some of the medieval musical instruments that have inspired the instruments we use today:

○ The **bladder pipe** is a simplified bagpipe, complete with a blow pipe, a chanter, a double reed and, yes, a bladder for a bag. Nice!

○ The **shawm** comes from the woodwind family and was a forerunner of the oboe – it certainly sounds like a reedier version of one. It looked a bit like a recorder but with a trumpet-like bell shape at the end. They came in several sizes, from soprano to bass.

o The **rebec** looks like a mini boat-shaped fiddle and was around as early as the eleventh century. It has various numbers of strings and can be played on the arm, under the chin or on the lap.

o The **citole** was shaped like a holly leaf and the four strings were plucked with a quill. It's thought that the cittern developed from the citole.

o The **gittern** looked more like a small lute, as did the pear-shaped **oud**.

One thing you can say about medieval musicians – they weren't short of a stringed instrument or two.

CLASSICAL CHUCKLES

Why do bagpipe players march when they play?
To get away from the sound.

> ### GRACE NOTE
>
> The earliest known musical instrument, the Divje Babe Flute, is thought to be from the Neanderthal era. Part of a cave bear femur pierced with holes, it was discovered in Slovenia in 1995.

THE MEDIEVAL MAID

HILDEGARD OF BINGEN (1098–1179)

Also known as Saint Hildegard, this Benedictine abbess, visionary, poet and philosopher was one of the earliest known composers. Hildegard was born into a noble German family and, as the tenth child, was offered into the Church as a tithe. At eight years old, she was sent as a novice to the Benedictine monastery of Disibodenberg.

From a very early age, Hildegard experienced visions and received a call from God to write them down. This she did, along with medicinal and scientific writings, and a significant output of music.

Among her compositions, the earliest surviving morality play *Ordo Virtutum* (*Order of the Virtues*) is probably one of her better known works, along with her other major work, a collection of liturgical songs, *Symphonia Armonie Celestium Revelationum* (*Symphony of the Harmony of Heavenly Revelations*), liturgical meaning music performed as part of a church service. The poetical texts of these songs reflect the visionary concept of her faith and are addressed variously to the Redeemer, the Blessed Virgin Mary and the Apostles.

Recommended listening

Ordo Virtutum tells of the battle between the Devil and the virtues to possess a lost soul. The work's single melody line is typical of monophonic music and it contains more than 80 separate melodies to accompany the words.

RENAISSANCE PERIOD: c.1400–1600

It's difficult to put an exact date on the start of the Renaissance Period, as it was out with the Middle Ages and in with a huge cultural and social rebirth which took years to evolve. Music continued to be very church-orientated, with the rise of the anthem, the mass and the motet (a form of sacred polyphonic vocal music, usually accompanied). Despite this, the Church was beginning to lose its stranglehold; witness the Reformation, and the freedom it brought, which inspired an enthusiastic interest in art, science, astronomy and mathematics.

This freedom began to be reflected musically. One of the most significant advances for the music of the period was the invention of the printing press in 1450 which meant music could be published, taking in a wider audience and helping to spread composers' reputations.

It was still mainly choral music, and based on modes, but polyphonic music continued to evolve and become more complicated, with three or four voice parts being added to new compositions to give a piece a richer, fuller texture. Harmony and chord progression began to have more flow, and some church music was accompanied by instruments – the development of instrumental music had begun.

The Renaissance saw an increase in secular music too, inspiring a rich variety of dances, instrumental and vocal pieces – notably *chansons* and madrigals (a part-song often set to a short poem, and usually about love), which were popular in Italy and France; the Italian composer Claudio Monteverdi wrote nine books of them.

Typical of this period, pieces of music were often accompanied by a consort, which was a group of musicians playing instruments of the same family but in different sizes – a whole consort. However, it could also be a broken consort, made up of different families of instruments such as viols, recorders and citterns.

Recommended listening

Monteverdi's music bridges the Renaissance and early baroque eras, so his *Vespers* is a good example of the progress music had made from the single, unaccompanied form of melody. The work includes soloists and choruses (with ten vocal parts at times) and is accompanied by strings, cornets and sackbuts. Expect lively rhythms and flowing melody.

And for accompaniment

o A **cornamuse** is a member of the woodwind family and, unlike the **crumhorn** (which is curved like a large grappling hook), is straight. Both have two reeds – as opposed to a saxophone or a clarinet, which has one – and unlike their modern counterparts, the reeds are housed in the windcap at the top of the instrument, not in the mouthpiece. They sound very similar to each other – very reedy – but the crumhorn has a deeper timbre.

o Invented around 1590, the **serpent** was named after its shape. Although it's classed as a wind instrument, it's related to the modern tuba – and sounds a bit like one too.

o The **sackbut** – translated from the old French *saquier* (to pull) and *bouter* (to push) – is a wind instrument that looks like a trombone.

o The **viol** or **viol da gamba,** which became one of the most popular Renaissance instruments, is a fretted stringed instrument that looks rather like a cello and is played between the legs. They were often played in consorts.

o Keyboard-like instruments, such as the **clavichord,** the **harpsichord** and the **virginal,** were making an appearance.

o A **rackett** is a double-reeded wind instrument, and looks like a cross between a stubby telescope and a blowtorch.

GRACE NOTE

Henry VIII was a talented musician and composer who owned a large collection of 78 flutes, 76 recorders, ten trombones, 14 trumpets and five bagpipes. Many of his compositions, including Masses and ballads, have been lost, although some of his songs, such as the jaunty 'Pastime with Good Company', are still performed today.

THE RENAISSANCE RAKES

PALESTRINA, GIOVANNI PIERLUIGI DA (c.1525–94)

This Italian Renaissance composer was a prolific writer of motets, Masses, hymns and madrigals. After a time as an organist and teacher, he ended up as singing master for the Cappella Giulia, the choir of Saint Peter's Basilica, a position later taken up by the baroque composer Scarlatti from 1715 to 1719.

His personal life was tragic and turbulent, losing his brother, two of his sons and then his wife to the plague. He apparently considered the priesthood but instead married a wealthy widow, which ensured his financial comfort while he composed.

Recommended listening

The smooth choral entrances and triumphant musical statements of the Gloria or the quieter, more restrained interweaving musical lines of the Kyrie from Palestrina's *Missa Papae Marcelli* (*Pope Marcellus Mass*) c.1555.

TALLIS, THOMAS (c.1505–85)

An English composer whose birthplace was probably in Kent, Tallis served several monarchs during his lifetime. He is best known for his church choral music, and given the religious ferments during his lifetime, he was obviously skilled at adapting his musical styles to suit both Catholic and Protestant tastes. Wise man.

From 1542, he entered royal service and was a Gentleman of the Chapel Royal, where he composed and performed music for Henry VIII, Edward VI, Queen Mary and Queen Elizabeth I, remaining there until his death in 1585. He shared the duties of chapel organist and composer with William Byrd, who was a pupil of Tallis.

Byrd and Tallis formed a business partnership in 1575 after Queen Elizabeth I granted them a 21-year patent to publish and print music. They published a collection of 34 *cantiones sacrae* (sacred songs) between them but they didn't sell very well.

Upon Tallis' death, Byrd wrote, 'Tallis is dead and music dies.'

Recommended listening

Sample his contrasting harmonic styles with the simple four-part anthem 'If Ye Love Me', then move on to the stunning 40-part devotional motet 'Spem in Alium' ('Hope in any Other').

MAIN MUSICAL FORMS

SONATA

The sonata in the baroque period was just a word to describe a piece of music that was played (the Italian *sonare* means 'to sound') rather than sung. In the following years, though, the word sonata took on a whole different interpretation.

The sonata really developed during the classical period (*c.*1750–1820), and at this time, came to mean a work in several movements (notably three or four), with the first movement itself in sonata form (see below).

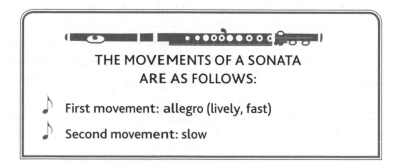

THE MOVEMENTS OF A SONATA ARE AS FOLLOWS:

♪ First movement: allegro (lively, fast)

♪ Second movement: slow

♪ Third movement: minuet and trio (or scherzo)

♪ Fourth movement: allegro

But it was the first movement, in sonata form, that marked a piece out as a classical composition. There are three main sections to this first movement:

♪ Exposition

♪ Development

♪ Recapitulation

The **exposition** presents, or exposes, if you will, the main theme or melody for the first time. But a second theme follows after this, and together they're called the **first subject** and the **second subject**.

The first subject is usually in the tonic (home) key and the second subject is in a different one, usually the dominant key (that is, a fifth up) or the relative minor (a third below). The connecting bridge passage(s) between these two themes is known as the **transition**, which is the part where it changes keys.

The next section is the **development** where the themes are explored and developed in different ways, for example, more key changes or even (sometimes) the introduction of a new snippet of melody.

In the **recapitulation,** the themes from the exposition are repeated, but the first subject might be a bit shorter than when first heard, and used a little differently. The movement may end in the tonic key, and there may be a coda (or tail), which is a small section of music that brings it to a satisfying close.

SYMPHONY

The word 'symphony' comes from the Greek *symphonia* which means 'sounding together'. The symphony really came into its own during the classical and baroque periods.

The standard form is:

o First movement: allegro (in sonata form)

o Second movement: slow (often quite simple, and in **ternary** form – see below)

o Third movement: minuet and trio

o Fourth movement: allegro

Ternary form

Ternary form, or song form, is a composition in three sections, the third section of which is a repetition of the first, so A, B, A.

CONCERTO GROSSO

This evolved over the seventeenth and eighteenth centuries and is a form of baroque music where a larger group of instruments (the ripieno) plays with a smaller group of solo instruments (the concertino). Bach's Brandenburg Concertos are a good example of this musical form.

CONCERTO

The concerto grosso had largely fallen out of favour by the beginning of the classical period; the concerto then emerging as the musical form we know today, that is as a single solo instrument (replacing the concertino) playing with an orchestra. There are usually three movements in a concerto.

CHAMBER MUSIC

Chamber music was, and is, written for small groups of musicians. Originally, it was played as a form of entertainment for friends and families in their own homes. Typical chamber music might be a piano trio, a string trio, or a quartet, which (unlike a full-blown orchestra) could be performed by only one player per part.

From the nineteenth century onwards, this music began to migrate to smaller concert halls, but it still carries the title of chamber music. The Wigmore Hall in London is a great example of a smaller venue that specialises in putting on chamber music.

FUGUE

This is music in which two or more independent melodies are woven together (also known as contrapuntal music or counterpoint). The melodic lines, often referred to as 'voices', can be either freely composed or written within an organised system. For instance, the original theme can be continued with a number of variations, while the whole is developed musically. This form of writing developed during the Renaissance Period, and Bach is the acclaimed master of the form. A good example of a fugue occurs in Mozart's 'Jupiter' symphony.

STRING QUARTET

A group of two violins, a viola and a cello, the string quartet is seen as one of the most important forms of chamber music. The music written for these quartets has a structure similar to that of a symphony, that is, in four movements. We have Josef Haydn to thank for the development of the string quartet, all the more remarkable that it came about almost by accident. Before Haydn began his long musical association with the Esterházy, he was employed for a while around 1755 by Austrian nobleman Karl Joseph von Fürnberg. The Baron wanted to hear some music, and the available instrumentalists happened to be two violinists, a violist and a cellist, so Haydn wrote a quartet for them.

GRACE NOTE

Morton Feldman (1926–87) was an American composer whose String Quartet No. 2, written in 1983, lasts for 6 hours and has been written as one continuous piece, with no movements. It is verrrry sloooww…

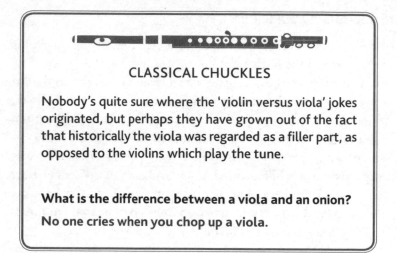

CLASSICAL CHUCKLES

Nobody's quite sure where the 'violin versus viola' jokes originated, but perhaps they have grown out of the fact that historically the viola was regarded as a filler part, as opposed to the violins which play the tune.

What is the difference between a viola and an onion?

No one cries when you chop up a viola.

MUSICAL EXPRESSIONS

Why are expressions in Italian? By the late sixteenth and early seventeenth centuries, many Italian Renaissance and baroque composers had begun to write instruction and expression marks on their compositions – and it's stuck.

The louds

Fortississimo (fff): very, very loud
Fortissimo (ff): very loud
Forte (f): loud
Fortepiano (fp): loud then immediately soft
Mezzo-forte (mf): moderately loud

The softs

Pianississimo (ppp): very, very soft
Pianissimo (pp): very soft

Mezzo-piano (mp): moderately soft
Piano (p): soft

The fasts

Prestissimo: very very fast
Presto: very fast
Allegro: lively, fast
Allegretto: a little fast (though not as fast as allegro)
Vivace: lively

The slows

Grave: very slow, solemn
Largo: very slow, broad
Larghetto: rather slow (but faster than largo)
Adagio: moderately slow
Lento: slow (but generally faster than adagio)
Andante: at a walking pace, i.e. a moderate tempo
Andantino: quicker than andante

A to Z

Accelerando: quickening the tempo
Ad libitum [Latin]: a passage performed freely, as the performer
   pleases
Agitato: agitated
Alla: in the style of
Allargando: broadening
Appassionato: with passion
Arco: with the bow
A tempo: in time (after a change of speed)
Ben marcato: well-marked
Brio: vigour

Calando: dying away
Cantabile: in a singing style
Capriccioso: in a whimsical or fanciful style
Con brio: with brightness
Con fuoco: with fire
Con moto: with speed
Crescendo: gradually getting louder
Da capo: from the beginning
Decrescendo: gradually getting softer
Diminuendo: gradually getting softer
Dolce: sweetly
Espressivo: expressively
Fine: the end
Giocoso: playful, humorous
Glissando: sliding
Grandioso: grandly
Lachrymose: sad
Largamente: broadly
Legato: smoothly, evenly
Leggiero: lightly
Maestoso: majestic
Ma non troppo: but not too much
Marcato: emphatic, accented
Meno: less
Moderato: moderate speed
Molto: much
Morendo: dying away
Mosso: in motion, animated
Ossia: or, alternatively (often to indicate a simpler version of a difficult passage)
Ostinato: a repeated theme or figure (if the theme is in the bass, it is referred to as ground bass)

Parlando: a passage performed as though speaking, for example a recitative

Pesante: heavily

Piacevole: pleasantly

Più: more

Pizzicato: plucked

Poco: a little

Rallentando: gradually getting slower

Recitative: a free style of singing, with the rhythms of dramatic speech

Ritenuto: held back, suddenly and temporarily

Scherzando: playful

Segue: follow on without a break

Sempre: always, e.g. 'sempre pesante', always heavily

Senza: without

Sforzando: strongly accented

Sostenuto: sustained

Sotto: below, e.g. 'sotto voce', in an undertone

Staccato: detached

Stringendo: gradually getting faster

Subito: suddenly

Tacet: silent (as in a musical part with nothing to play for a section)

Tempo: speed

Tempo rubato: 'robbed time' – with some freedom of time, that is, certain passages of music played at a faster or slower tempo

Tenuto: held (usually notes or chords)

Troppo: too much

Tutti: everyone

Veloce: swift

Vivo: lively

Volante: fast and light

MUSIC THROUGH
THE AGES:
PART TWO

BAROQUE PERIOD: c.1600–1750

Translated from the French, the word *baroque* means 'elaborate',
so it might well have first been used in the derogatory sense,
as new and more complex musical forms began to take
shape. Certainly, the period was known for its extravagantly
decorated architecture which was reflected musically with trills,
embellishments and ornamentation.

But most significantly, this was the time when a good many
of the foundations of Western music had their beginnings and
instrumental music began to take on as important a role as
vocal music.

Harmonies were becoming more complicated – more recognisable
as those that we hear today – as were melody lines. But what
really put the baroque period on the map was the development
of a form of accompaniment called basso continuo or continuous
bass (also known simply as continuo) that was played by a

keyboard instrument such as a harpsichord. The composer would write a single note on the bottom line (that is, the bass (see Glossary) line played by the left hand), and would indicate what the harmony should be, as well as which chords should be played, by writing figured instructions underneath the music. These instructions were known as figured bass. A bit like musical shorthand.

Dramatic music such as opera, cantata (see Glossary) and oratorio made an appearance, as did the embryonic sonata and the concerto grosso. With the rise of instrumental music came the beginnings of the orchestra, though the baroque orchestra was pretty small by today's standards.

Recommended listening

Johann Sebastian Bach's Brandenburg Concerto No. 5 in D Major has baroque figured bass and plenty of scope for the flute, violin and harpsichord to show off.

Antonio Vivaldi's Mandolin Concerto in C Major, as well as other pieces of his music, explored the new instruments of the era, including the oboe, the clarinet and the mandolin.

And for accompaniment

Instrument names are becoming more familiar...

o The **harpsichord** functioned as a bass line provider, elbowing out the softer **clavichord** which couldn't be heard in ensembles.

o The **violin** appeared (superseding the viol and its role as a consort instrument), striking out as a solo instrument.

o The **flute** had been around since Roman times in a simple form, but it became a three-piece instrument during the middle 1600s, pitched in the key of D, and is an ancestor of the flute we hear today.

o The **hautboy** was the oboe of the baroque period. It too underwent technical changes during this time, and was the first of the woodwind instruments to be played alongside stringed instruments to form a new kind of ensemble, from which the first small orchestra was born.

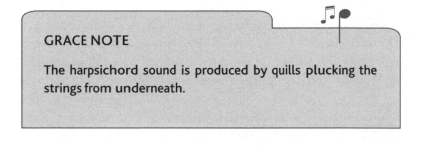

GRACE NOTE

The harpsichord sound is produced by quills plucking the strings from underneath.

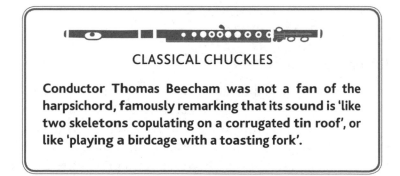

CLASSICAL CHUCKLES

Conductor Thomas Beecham was not a fan of the harpsichord, famously remarking that its sound is 'like two skeletons copulating on a corrugated tin roof', or like 'playing a birdcage with a toasting fork'.

THE BAROQUE BOYS

PURCELL, HENRY (1659-95)

> 'Mr Purcell, in whose person we have at length
> found an Englishman equal with the best
> abroad.'

JOHN DRYDEN

Purcell was another stalwart of the Chapel Royal, being a chorister there. He was a keyboard virtuoso and studied with composer John Blow, until he took over Blow's job as organist at Westminster Abbey when he was only 20 years old. As well as his royal duties as court composer, writing anthems, odes and celebratory pieces, Purcell is probably best remembered for his later works for the stage, in particular his operas *Dido and Aeneas* and *The Fairy Queen*. It is said that the music he wrote for Queen Mary's funeral in 1695 was subsequently played at his own, in the same year.

Recommended listening

Many a bride has walked down the aisle to Purcell's 'Trumpet Voluntary', and for a complete contrast, Dido's aria, 'When I Am Laid in Earth', from the opera *Dido and Aeneas*, uses a technique known as ground bass (a short, continuously repeating bass theme) to great effect, giving musical emphasis to Dido's overwhelming sense of grief.

> ♪♪
>
> ## GRACE NOTE
>
> *Dido and Aeneas* was first performed at Josias Priest's Chelsea School for Young Ladies, in London, in *c*.1688.

VIVALDI, ANTONIO (1678–1741)

Vivaldi was born on 4 March 1678 in Venice, during an earthquake. He struggled with illness throughout his life and was always sickly, his symptoms now being interpreted as asthma. Vivaldi is thought of as a composer first and foremost, but it is sometimes forgotten that he was also a virtuoso violinist, his father having taught him to play as a child.

He was ordained into the priesthood in 1703, his red hair earning him the nickname *il prete rosso* (the red priest). That same year he was appointed violin teacher at the Ospedale della Pietà, an orphanage and music school in Venice. His association with the school lasted the rest of his life, and it was while he was there that he wrote most of his major works, including concertos and violin sonatas.

Vivaldi also had a great love of opera and his first composition, *Ottone in Villa* (*Otho at his Villa*), premiered in 1713. He was voted out of office by the Pietà's governors, in March 1716, for spending too much time composing operas, but by May that same year, he was voted back in. He does, then, seem to have been allowed to work on his operas and other works away from the school, as he spent much of the latter part of his life on the move.

Not many people can hum a Vivaldi opera but it is Vivaldi's concertos – and the contribution that he made to the baroque era with these – that have endured. His output was staggering:

more than 400 concertos, plus his Glorias, cantatas and around 45 operas, although he may have written many more.

Recommended listening

There's a lot more to Vivaldi than just his violin concerto *Le Quattro Stagioni* (*The Four Seasons*), although it is a work of art. Try the opening movement to his Gloria, with its joyful, exuberant octaves (see Glossary) and semiquavers.

Also, one or two of Vivaldi's Six Flute Concertos, Op. 10, for flute, strings and basso continuo, is a fine way to spend an evening.

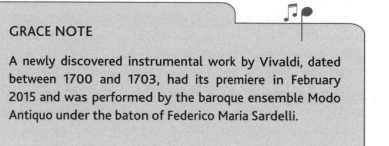

GRACE NOTE

A newly discovered instrumental work by Vivaldi, dated between 1700 and 1703, had its premiere in February 2015 and was performed by the baroque ensemble Modo Antiquo under the baton of Federico Maria Sardelli.

BACH, JOHANN SEBASTIAN (1685-1750)

Like Vivaldi, Bach was another prolific musician, although he obviously put his pen down now and then as he had 20 children, sadly of whom only ten survived.

He was born in Eisenach, Germany, where his father was the town's musical director, so it was probably he who taught his son to play the violin and harpsichord. Bach was orphaned when he was ten years old and he went to live with his elder brother, Johann Christoph, who was an organist, and who taught his younger sibling the clavichord.

Blessed with a fine voice, Bach was awarded a choral scholarship to St Michael's School in Lüneburg, but it was in playing the school's organ and harpsichord that he found his great love. His technical skill at the keyboard landed him a position in 1703 as organist at a church in Arnstadt. While there, he began composing in earnest and took several months off – without permission – to travel to hear the great composer and organist Dieterich Buxtehude. Bach, it seemed, was a man who did exactly what he wanted.

Bach's time as organist at the court of Wilhelm Ernst, Duke of Saxe-Weimar, began in 1708 and marked a period of intense composition – church cantatas, and keyboard, organ and orchestral works. Eventually, he fell foul of Ernst and landed in jail for a month before being given his marching orders.

Not the slightest bit daunted, he went to the court of Leopold, Prince of Anhalt-Köthen, in 1717 to serve as his director of music. Bach's compositions during this time were prolific – lots of secular music, including the Brandenburg Concertos, his double violin concerto, sonatas for harpsichord and flute, and suites for cello and violin.

He moved to Leipzig in 1723, taking up the post of organist and director of church music at St Thomas Church, writing cantatas and the big ones – *St John Passion*, *St Matthew Passion*, the *Christmas Oratorio* and the Mass in B Minor, written one year before his death in 1750.

Recommended listening

Bach's Double Violin Concerto in D Minor; the second movement is a moving, lyrical passing of phrases between two violins, which is sublime and Bach at his absolute best.

HANDEL, GEORGE FRIDERIC (1685-1759)

Ah, *Water Music*, *Music for the Royal Fireworks*, how very British. Well, yes and no – Handel was born in Halle, Germany, although you might be forgiven for thinking he was born in England, as he spent a good deal of his musical career there and he was laid to rest in Westminster Abbey.

Handel was master of the baroque oratorio, opera and anthem, but unlike Bach, he didn't have a musical family to encourage his talents. His father, who was a surgeon, wanted him to study law and was appalled that Handel took such a keen interest in music. But the young man persisted and showed such prodigious talent at the keyboard that by the time he was 17, Handel was organist at Halle Cathedral.

But his love lay with opera, and in 1703, he was drawn to Hamburg, Germany's operatic centre, where he composed his first operas, *Almira* and *Nero*, which both premiered in 1705. In 1706, his operatic yearnings led him to Italy. There Handel was the guest of the members of the Italian aristocracy, including the Medici family, and his operas *Rodrigo* (1707) and *Aggripina* (1709) were very well received.

The House of Hanover was interested in securing Handel's services, and in 1710, Handel was appointed *kapellmeister* (the leader or conductor of an orchestra or choir) to George, the Elector of Hanover. Handel drove a hard bargain in his negotiations of the position, angling for a good salary and the option to take 12 months off. Quite a businessman, some might say, but it was a deal that was to cause friction later on.

Within six months of taking on his new position, Handel left for London, where his next opera, *Rinaldo*, was a huge success. He returned briefly to Hanover in June 1711 but by the autumn of 1712 he was given permission to come back to London for a short while – and he never returned to Hanover. Queen Anne gave him a yearly pension of £200 and, in return, he composed *Utrecht Te Deum and Jubilate* for her.

When Queen Anne died in 1714, Handel's frustrated employer, the Elector of Hanover, took the throne, becoming King George I of Great Britain. It is said, however, that Handel was forgiven, and King George continued to employ this brightest of baroque composers. Perhaps the 1717 *Water Music*, composed for King George's procession along the River Thames, was an offering designed to pour oil on troubled waters.

And so began years of creative work – operas such as *Giulio Cesare* (1724), *Tamerlano* (1724) and *Rodelinda* (1725); the anthem 'Zadok the Priest', composed for the coronation of King George II in 1727 (and, incidentally, played at every British coronation since); the oratorios *Messiah* and *Samson* (both 1741), *Judas Maccabaeus* (1746) and *Solomon* (1748). His last major work was *Music for the Royal Fireworks*, written to accompany the fireworks in Green Park to celebrate the signing of the Treaty of Aix-la-Chappelle in 1748.

Recommended listening

The soprano solo 'Let the Bright Seraphim' from Handel's oratorio *Samson*. The sparkling musical interplay between soprano and solo trumpet will give you an inkling of Handel's genius. Joan Sutherland's version is hard to beat.

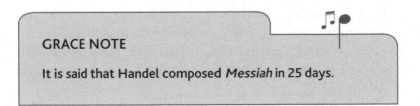

GRACE NOTE

It is said that Handel composed *Messiah* in 25 days.

CLASSICAL PERIOD: c.1750-1820

Music from all these periods is described as classical, but it is the era from the mid 1700s to the early 1800s (remarkably only around 60 years) which is defined as the classical period – perhaps because so much of what was written can be considered 'classic', in no small part due to the prolific output of the big three, Mozart, Haydn and Beethoven, who were all active during this time.

The Church became less of an influence, as music gained momentum in courts, and if you were a composer of note, royal commissions would come your way, leading to many composers going 'freelance' by the end of the period.

Music became simpler and clearer; formality, elegance, beauty and balance were the watchwords. There was greater variety in dynamics, rhythms and keys, and a more structured elegance to the writing; less ornamentation (no more improvisations allowed!) and more of a natural, expressive outlook musically.

The music may have been less ornate but the orchestra, and the sound it made, was increasing in size and volume. Instrumental music – the symphony, concerto, wind and string pieces (in particular chamber music for quartets) – all put in an appearance, and the sonata was an important development.

Recommended listening

From its intense opening four-note sequence and the violins' scurrying semiquavers, Mozart's Symphony No. 25 in G Minor is a work full of drama, grace and clever changes of mood.

Haydn's String Quartet, Op. 1, No. 1, in B-flat Major has an opening romp, a graceful minuet, wistful melodies and a cracking finish.

And, finally, what better than Beethoven's Fifth Symphony for passion and power.

And for accompaniment

o The **piano** was rapidly overtaking the harpsichord, with sonatas being composed for various solo instruments and the piano.

o The **clarinet** appeared in the orchestra for the first time.

o Most of the instruments of the modern orchestra had appeared by the 1820s, although the tuba and the lower woodwind instruments had yet to put in an appearance.

CLASSICAL CHAMPIONS

HAYDN, FRANZ JOSEPH (1732-1809)

Austrian Joseph Haydn was born when both Handel and Bach were at the height of their musical powers. He is regarded as contributing many of the pivotal musical forms which provided the basis of the classical period of music – the symphony, the string quartet, the concerto and the sonata. Heralded as 'Papa Haydn', he is still regarded as the 'father of the symphony' and the 'father of the string quartet' (writing 83 of the latter).

Haydn's father was a wheelwright but he was also an amateur musician, and it was he who realised very early on that Haydn had something special musically. By the age of around seven or eight, he was enrolled at the choir school at St Stephen's Cathedral in Vienna. However, in 1749, he was abruptly dismissed when his voice broke and, it is said, he cut off the pigtail of a fellow chorister. Exit Haydn.

His early years as a freelance musician were a struggle. He made only a meagre living by taking what jobs he could as a music teacher and accompanist, and had to teach himself music theory and composition along the way. In 1760, Haydn married Maria Anna Keller, but it is well documented that their marriage was not a happy one. His wife had no appreciation of his music and they had no children.

However, things started to look up in 1761 when Haydn was offered a job as musical director with the immensely rich Esterházy family, an association that was to last nearly 30 years. He ran the musical household, and rehearsed and conducted the orchestra, but above all, he composed for the Esterházy princes' pleasure, and his musical output was huge – symphonies, operettas, string quartets, dance music and a lot of opera.

Haydn may have felt overworked but he surely realised the remarkable opportunity he had been given to compose to his heart's content in such a rarefied musical environment, something which, given his prodigious output, he used to his full advantage. 'I was cut off from the world... I was forced to become original.'

Haydn did take the opportunity to travel now and then; he visited Vienna a number of times and a great bond of friendship developed between himself and Mozart. Haydn wrote to Mozart's father, Leopold, 'I tell you before God... that your son is the greatest composer known to me by person and repute.'

Haydn was released from his contract in 1790, and he travelled to London in 1791, finding that his musical fame had preceded him. His two periods in London coincided with the writing of some of his best works, including his 12 London symphonies (including 'Surprise' and 'The Clock').

King George III tried to persuade Haydn to stay in England but he returned to Vienna in 1795, again serving the Esterházys, and it was during this latter period of his life that he composed his two great oratorios *The Creation* (1798) and *The Seasons* (1801).

While Haydn was in England, it is said he was impressed with the British national anthem. Upon his return to Vienna, he wrote a hymn for Emperor Francis II's birthday, 'Gott Erhalte Franz den Kaiser' ('God Save Emperor Franz'), the tune being adopted by Germany after 1922 as its national anthem. The theme is also present in the second movement of his String Quartet, Op. 76, No. 3 ('Emperor'); one of six that he wrote around 1796.

From 1802, Haydn's health began to deteriorate, and he made his last public appearance at a concert in Vienna in March 1808, when Salieri conducted a performance of *The Creation*. He lay dying in May 1809 as Napoleon's troops attacked Vienna.

Recommended listening

Play the second movement of the 'Surprise' Symphony, No. 94 in G Major and listen to the lyrical violins for about 16 bars, before the surprise appears. 'I was interested in surprising the public with something new.'

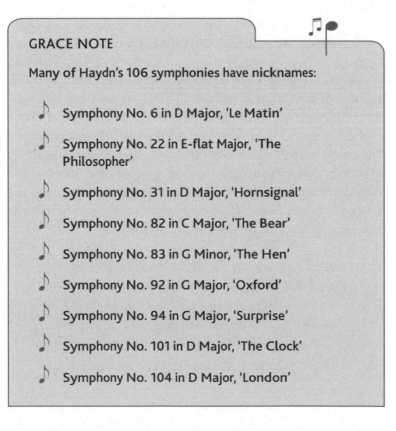

GRACE NOTE

Many of Haydn's 106 symphonies have nicknames:

- Symphony No. 6 in D Major, 'Le Matin'
- Symphony No. 22 in E-flat Major, 'The Philosopher'
- Symphony No. 31 in D Major, 'Hornsignal'
- Symphony No. 82 in C Major, 'The Bear'
- Symphony No. 83 in G Minor, 'The Hen'
- Symphony No. 92 in G Major, 'Oxford'
- Symphony No. 94 in G Major, 'Surprise'
- Symphony No. 101 in D Major, 'The Clock'
- Symphony No. 104 in D Major, 'London'

MOZART, WOLFGANG AMADEUS (1756–91)

'My children have taken everyone by storm.'
**LEOPOLD MOZART WRITING TO CHRISTIAN VON MECHEL
IN DECEMBER 1763**

Mozart: the child prodigy, the man, the music and the mystery. Miloš Forman's 1984 film adaptation of Peter Shaffer's play, *Amadeus*, opened up the intriguing possibility that Mozart was poisoned by composer Antonio Salieri – but that's just one theory said by those who love a good story. What the film did do, however, was to introduce Mozart to a new audience, and for those already familiar with his works, to reignite the love affair.

Born in Salzburg, Mozart was already picking out chords (see Glossary) on the clavier by the time he was three. Two years on, he was studying the keyboard with his violinist father, Leopold, and composing his first minuet. In 1763, father, son and older sister Maria Anna (nicknamed 'Nannerl') embarked on a tour of the European courts to show off the two Mozart prodigies. They were a huge success, feted by royalty and the aristocracy wherever they performed, but the touring was intense and arduous. They were away from Salzburg for three years, and Mozart was composing as well as performing. By the time he was ten, Mozart had written his first symphonies.

*'Four sonatas by Monsieur Wolfgang Mozart
are currently being engraved. Just imagine the
stir that these sonatas will make in the world
when it says on the title page that they are
the work of a seven-year-old child.'*
LEOPOLD MOZART TO MARIA THERESIA HAGENAUER

In December 1769, during a two-year tour of Italy, Mozart received his first opera commission, *Mitridate, re di Ponto*, which was a triumphant success and which reaffirmed his extraordinary talent as a composer as well as a performer.

Mozart returned to Salzburg in 1773, and over the next few years was employed as *konzertmeister* by the ruler of Salzburg. He wasn't happy – after having been honoured and petted over as a prodigy by the crowned heads of Europe, the flamboyant composer found life with the dour Cardinal Archbishop, Count Hieronymus von Colloredo, difficult to cope with. It didn't stop him from composing five violin concertos and any number of symphonies including the fabulous Symphony No. 25 in G Minor, the dramatic beginning of which was used as the opening music in *Amadeus*, which Mozart wrote when he was only 17. Add to that a bassoon concerto, various divertimenti (light-hearted instrumental pieces), minuets and several Masses, Mozart must have had permanently ink-stained fingers.

Further tours followed, and so his employer had to grudgingly give the increasingly unhappy Mozart time off to go to Vienna and Munich. By August 1777, desperate to get away from Salzburg, Mozart resigned from his position at the court. The Archbishop's response was to sack both him and his father, Leopold, who was deputy *kapellmeister*; he did, however, relent and allow Leopold back into the fold.

Mozart needed to find employment and so, accompanied by his mother, he began the search, visiting Mannheim, Munich and Paris; it was while they were in Paris that his mother died.

Summoned back to Salzburg by his father, Mozart took up service at court again, as the organist, in January 1780. By the summer he had received a commission for an opera from the Elector of Bavaria, and *Idomeneo* premiered with great success in Munich. The Archbishop ordered Mozart to Vienna, where his relationship with his employer deteriorated further, and

FOR THE LOVE OF CLASSICAL MUSIC

Mozart was dismissed with a boot on the backside from the Archbishop's steward, Count Arco.

But that kick changed Mozart's life, and for the first time he was free. He travelled to Vienna and began teaching piano while setting about raising his musical profile. He established himself (once again) as a fine keyboard player, and in July 1782, his opera *Die Entführung aus dem Serail* (*The Abduction from the Seraglio*) premiered to huge acclaim. The opera '… has knocked everything else sideways,' stated the German writer Johann Wolfgang von Goethe.

Barely a month later, Mozart married Constanze Weber and the marriage, by all accounts, was a happy one; they had six children, of whom only two survived infancy. It seems that marital contentment might have contributed to his great outpouring of composition during his Viennese years: symphonies, piano concertos, violin sonatas and other chamber music – not least his set of six string quartets dedicated to his great friend Joseph Haydn.

> '*Here they are then, O great man and my dearest
> friend, these six children of mine…
> the fruit of long and laborious work.*'

Opera was a major force in Mozart's life and after the success of *Idomeneo* and *Die Entführung aus dem Serail* came what some consider to be two of his greatest operas, *Le nozze di Figaro* (*The Marriage of Figaro*) in 1785 and *Don Giovanni* in 1787.

The trouble was that with success came ill-advised spending; the Mozarts were living beyond their means and his financial success didn't last long. Mozart did, however, find a permanent position in 1787 when Emperor Joseph II appointed him chamber composer after the death of Christoph Willibald Gluck, but it came with only a modest salary.

Although the last years of his life were plagued with illness, it didn't prevent him from embarking on concert tours to Germany, and his prodigious rate of composition slowed only a little. This last period marked some of his finest works: three symphonies, including his last, 'Jupiter'; his operas *Così fan Tutte* (*The School for Lovers*) and *Die Zauberflöte* (*The Magic Flute*); and his wonderful clarinet concerto in A Major.

He was commissioned to compose a requiem, but he never finished it, and the ebullient Mozart died on 5 December 1791. Constanze's sister, Sophie, recounts Mozart's final hours:

> *'Suessmayr was at Mozart's bedside. The well-known Requiem lay on the quilt, and Mozart was explaining to him how, in his opinion, he ought to finish it, when he was gone... the last thing he did was to try and mouth the drum passages in the Requiem. I can still hear that.'*

Recommended listening

The soprano solo, 'Alleluia', from the motet 'Exsultate, Jubilate', which he composed towards the end of a stay in Italy in 1772, has a fast, brightly lyrical melody which calls for great control from the singer.

By contrast, the slow, powerful Commendatore's bass-baritone solo from act two of Mozart's opera *Don Giovanni* is a doom-laden message to warn Giovanni of his impending demise.

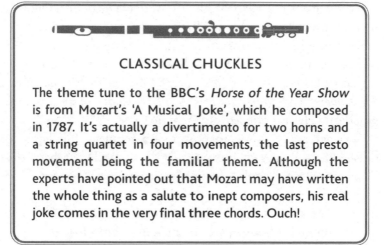

CLASSICAL CHUCKLES

The theme tune to the BBC's *Horse of the Year Show* is from Mozart's 'A Musical Joke', which he composed in 1787. It's actually a divertimento for two horns and a string quartet in four movements, the last presto movement being the familiar theme. Although the experts have pointed out that Mozart may have written the whole thing as a salute to inept composers, his real joke comes in the very final three chords. Ouch!

BEETHOVEN, LUDWIG VAN (1770–1827)

Barely a year after the death of Mozart, a young German musician left his native Bonn and arrived in the city of Vienna to study with Haydn. That young man was Beethoven, the musical giant who formed the bridge between the classical and Romantic periods. His turbulent story is every bit as fascinating as Mozart's, and is one of triumph over adversity.

He was born into a musical family, his grandfather having been music director to the Archbishop-Elector of Cologne, and his father Johann, a court musician. Johann was a harsh man and a drunkard who – once he realised his son's talent at the keyboard – drilled him unmercifully on seeing the financial advantages of exploiting his exceptional talent.

However, around Beethoven's ninth birthday, the organist at the Bonn court, Christian Gottlob Neefe, took Beethoven under his wing, continuing his musical training and teaching him composition. By 1783, Beethoven had already written three piano sonatas.

Vienna, however, was the place to go to progress musically and it is said that 17-year-old Beethoven went there in order to study with Mozart in 1787, but this has never been substantiated. Certainly, he received news that his mother was gravely ill and he returned home. She died of tuberculosis in July that same year.

As his father descended further into drink, Beethoven became the family breadwinner. To make ends meet, Beethoven gave piano lessons and played at court, where his musical talents gained him an influential patron, Count Ferdinand Waldstein. In fact, it was this same man who is said to have persuaded the Elector to let Beethoven go and study with Haydn in Vienna. By all accounts, these lessons were not a great success – a clash of characters, perhaps, with the old master Haydn and the up-and-coming fiery young man with few social graces. However, tensions aside, Beethoven quickly established a name for himself as a piano virtuoso, with a great reputation for improvising.

Supported by noble patronage, he gave his first public concert in 1795, playing one of his own piano concertos. From that point, his reputation as a composer and his portfolio grew with six string quartets between 1798 and 1800, his first and second symphonies, and a number of piano sonatas and concertos.

His prolific output was surely due to the fact that he knew his time left as a pianist was short, for around 1796 he became aware that he was losing his hearing. In 1802 Beethoven went to Heiligenstadt to rest and, while there, wrote his Heiligenstadt Testament, a letter written to his brothers, documenting his despair, the isolation his deafness had already brought and his thoughts of death:

'Oh ye men who accuse me of being malevolent, stubborn... how ye wrong me!... for six years I have been hopelessly ill... I was forced to isolate myself. I was misunderstood and rudely repulsed because I

was yet unable to say... "Speak louder, shout for I
am deaf"... With joy I hasten to meet death.'

The letter was never sent but it was found among his possessions after he died.

It is this struggle with his physical disability that is reflected in his major works of the next few years. By the time he composed his third symphony, the mighty *Sinfonia Eroica,* it was clear that Beethoven was breaking the 'safe' classical musical boundaries, introducing dissonances (see Glossary) and dramatic key changes; the fire and passion so characteristic of the Beethoven we know.

Disappointed with the lukewarm response to his only opera, *Fidelio,* in 1805, he concentrated on orchestral work including string quartets; his only violin concerto; and, in 1808, his Symphony No. 6, Op. 68, in F Major ('Pastorale') – a nod to Romanticism if ever there was one.

Although sacred music never figured large in Beethoven's output, his *Missa Solemnis*, composed over some years from 1819, is regarded as one of his crowning achievements, along with his Symphony No. 9 in D Minor ('Choral') in 1824.

From 1825 illness marred his life, although he continued composing. One of the last compositions before he died, his *Grosse Fuge* string quartet, is an extraordinary piece of work. More Stravinsky than Beethoven, it is modern, clashing, fiery and, perhaps, a final frustrated scream in defiance of his world of deafness.

Beethoven died in March 1827; his funeral was attended by a crowd of 20,000 people.

Recommended listening

Romance No. 2 in F Major for violin and piano – delicate and moving, it will raise the hairs on the back of your neck.

> **GRACE NOTE**
>
> Franz Schubert, whose own death followed soon after Beethoven's, was one of the torchbearers at his funeral.

SCHUBERT, FRANZ PETER (1797–1828)

Schubert, the bespectacled Austrian who died at the age of only 31, was a composer of the late classical period and the early Romantic period. Although the principle classical-period composers are deemed to be Haydn, Mozart and Beethoven (the 'big three'), Schubert should be included here, as he uses many of the classic musical forms, even though his songs are melodiously Romantic. He bridges the gap between the two periods.

Born in Vienna, Schubert and his three brothers were taught music by their schoolmaster father. Franz showed exceptional talent, playing the piano, the violin and the organ, which caught the attention of Antonio Salieri, and in 1808, he won a scholarship to the Imperial Seminary, where he learned harmony with the great composer and played in the school orchestra.

The Schubert family was poor and so Franz eventually returned home in 1814 to teach in his father's school. However, this didn't stop him composing five string quartets, three symphonies and an opera, and over the next two years he wrote well over 200 songs (perhaps as a result of the unrequited love of singer Therese Grob) including 'Gretchen am Spinnrade' ('Gretchen at the Spinning Wheel') and 'Der Erlkönig' ('The Erl-king') from the namesake poem by Goethe. Schubert was obviously fond of Goethe's poetry as he used his texts for more than 70 of his songs.

Schubert finally left home in 1816, and he devoted himself to composition, being very disciplined in his work: 'I compose every morning, and when one piece is done, I begin another.' The beautiful songs 'An die Musik' ('To Music') and 'Die Forelle' ('The Trout') were composed during this period – not to be confused with his 'Trout' Quintet which he composed in 1819.

By 1818 he was employed as music teacher to the wealthy Count Esterházy's daughters. Compared to the drudgery of teaching in his father's school, this new job felt like heaven to Schubert: 'I live and compose like a God.' He was becoming well known as a composer but a foolish decision to sell the copyright of some of his music, his frustrations as an operatic composer (none of his stage works were a success), and his failing health, took its toll. Adding to that, he started a symphony in 1822, which he never finished.

In his later years, Schubert, battling illness and depression, produced a prolific amount of breathtakingly darker music, such as his wonderful song cycle *Die schöne Müllerin* (*The Fair Maid of the Mill*), the gloomily powerful *Winterreise* (*Winter Journey*), plus chamber music, two piano trios and the great String Quintet in C Major.

He died of typhus in 1828, as a result of drinking dirty water.

Recommended listening

The String Quintet in C Major, D 956 – lyrical, moving, and has a violin melody line that soars.

GRACE NOTE

Considering his short life, Schubert wrote an extraordinary number of songs, more than 600. Even today, he is considered a master of the genre.

MUSIC, MUSIC, MUSIC: THE BIG WORKS

Favourite classical pieces are always a source of great discussion and everyone's definitive list will be different, as it should be. However, this selection of symphonies and chamber music will hopefully inspire you to add to your classical music collection.

SYMPHONIES

SYMPHONY NO. 5, BEETHOVEN

Topping the list of many people's favourites will be Beethoven's Fifth Symphony. Begun in the autumn of 1807, it took him some time to complete; both his fifth and his sixth symphonies were heard in public for the first time in December 1808. This symphony is Beethoven at his towering best. Its well-known C Minor four-note opening phrase – three short notes and one long – is Morse code for V, and was played on the timpani to provide the BBC's station identification for broadcasting services to Europe during the Second World War.

The notes are said to represent fate knocking at the door, and they could certainly represent the composer's battle with deafness that had begun to blight his composing. But the key moves to C Major later on in the movement, suggesting that Beethoven was not to be beaten, his music a symbol that hope springs eternal.

SYMPHONY NO. 3 IN E-FLAT MAJOR ('HEROIC'), BEETHOVEN

Many will say that Beethoven's 'Heroic' Symphony, composed in 1804, is the masterpiece of his career – after all, the man himself called the work heroic. However, sometimes the story of how it so very nearly became the 'Napoleon Bonaparte' Symphony runs the risk of overshadowing what a mighty piece of work it is. And, like all stories, time may have embellished it in the telling.

The young Corsican Napoleon Bonaparte had risen through the military ranks with astonishing speed – by 1792, at the age of 23, he was already a captain. Following the bloody French Revolution and the dispatch of Louis XVI and Marie Antoinette in 1793, and with shock waves reverberating around Europe's nobility, Napoleon continued his upward rise, taking command of the French army of Italy in 1796, at the age of only 27. By 1800 he was installed as France's first consul – his control over the country was growing.

Beethoven, the free spirit, was a big Bonaparte fan. In Napoleon, Beethoven saw a champion of the people, a hero of the common man – in effect, the embodiment of the Romantic ideal. His *Eroica* Symphony was inspired by the principles of the French Revolution, and to this end, he dedicated it to Napoleon as The *Bonaparte* Symphony.

However, in December 1804 came the news that Napoleon – the defender of the people – had declared himself emperor. In a fury, Beethoven scrubbed out the dedication to Napoleon, and tore off the title page, considering him now to be a tyrant. But the subtitle, 'Composed to celebrate the memory of a great man' is nevertheless left in, so perhaps another theory – that he changed the dedication in order not to risk losing his composition fee due from a royal patron – is one worth credence too.

The *Eroica* is a symphony of massive scope and depth, and nearly twice as long as a conventional symphony, the first movement alone being almost the same length as an entire Haydn work. In it, Beethoven used dissonances and syncopation (see Glossary) that completely threw the rulebook out of the window. The second movement is a funeral march of massive proportions, richly textured and layered with climaxes aplenty. The fabulous vivace of the third movement leads to the allegro molto of the fourth movement, with its theme and variations (a main melody followed by lots of versions of it) – and what a climax, with the brass section and strings orchestra at full tilt.

SYMPHONY NO. 9 IN D MINOR ('CHORAL'), BEETHOVEN

With his final symphony, composed between 1822 and 1824, Beethoven again broke new ground by adding a chorus, the first major composer to do so. He had wanted to put German poet Freidrich Schiller's poem 'Ode to Joy' to music for some time and incorporated it into the final movement, with four vocal soloists and a chorus.

By the time Beethoven finished composing the symphony, he had gone completely deaf. Despite his deafness, he insisted on conducting it and there is a poignant story of the great composer having to be turned round to acknowledge the cheers of the audience at its premiere.

SYMPHONY NO. 41 IN C ('JUPITER'), MOZART

'Jupiter' is one of Mozart's most exuberant symphonies – there are jokes, it's fun, and there's a phrase that seems to come from his *Eine Kleine Nachtmusik*. Incredibly, he wrote his last three symphonies in just six weeks.

This symphony is a good example of typical classical symphonic form – four movements, the first and fourth of which are written in a quick tempo, the second is slower, and the third is a minuet and trio (a dance movement with three beats in a bar).

The first movement of 'Jupiter' starts with wonderful question-and-answer phrases from the strings, the second is more subdued, with subtly interweaving changes of mood, and there's a beautifully lyrical third-movement minuet. You can tell from the fourth movement that Mozart was interested in the works of Bach because there are plenty of Bach's specialities, counterpoint and fugue in it. Clever chap.

SYMPHONY NO. 9, MAHLER

Mahler died in 1911, aged only 50. Although he had started on his tenth symphony, the ninth symphony was the last he completed and sadly he never lived to hear the first performance of it.

The end of his life was fraught with difficulties. He'd exhausted himself through overwork in Vienna, his daughter died from scarlet fever in 1907 and that same year he discovered that he had an incurable heart condition. 'The symphony must be like the world,' said Mahler, and Mahler's world was falling apart.

The symphony, the 'dark night of the soul' (as musician and music scholar Deryck Cooke termed it), certainly explores the terrifying nature of death but, until you reach the fourth movement, it's definitely not a depressing body of work – just listen to the rustic dances in the second movement.

It is the last few minutes of the last movement that are so very moving, the threads of the strings unwilling to let go of the threads of life that Mahler was struggling to grasp on to. The last movement is a resolution and a goodbye but the symphony is one that will not fade away to the next life without a fight.

SYMPHONY NO. 4 IN A MAJOR, OP. 90 ('ITALIAN'), MENDELSSOHN

The composer himself called this symphony the 'jolliest piece I have ever done'. This was a work inspired by the German composer's travels in Europe from 1829 to 1831, and it was finished in 1833. Mendelssohn didn't find the writing of it particularly 'jolly' as he penned several revisions, and, never satisfied, it wasn't published until after his death.

The joyous allegro vivace first movement gives way to a quieter, graceful and infinitely soothing minor key second movement. The third movement is a trio, and in the fourth presto movement you can definitely hear the Italian influence in the tarantella (Italian folk dance) theme.

SYMPHONY NO. 6 IN B MINOR ('PATHÉTIQUE'), TCHAIKOVSKY

This is the composer's final symphony, written in 1893, and was named by Tchaikovsky's brother. Contrary to much that has been written on the subject of his state of mind, Tchaikovsky saw this symphony as a culmination of his powers as a composer – it may be about death but not necessarily his own. In fact, in letters to his publisher and his nephew, he seemed rather upbeat about the writing of it.

Moving and lyrical, especially the beautiful stringed theme about six minutes in to the first movement; but then there's a real shock of noise and upset about five minutes further on when the timpani and brass get stuck in. This is a symphony marked by a battle of violent contrasts.

The second movement, in a peaceful three-four time, calms things down a little, leading to the march-like third movement which ends in a blaze of triumph. The fourth movement comes as a departure from the usual form, however. It's an adagio (slow) movement – normally the final movement would be an allegro (fast) one. The last few slow pulsing notes bring the symphony to a hushed and dramatic end.

GRACE NOTE

British composer Havergal Brian's 'Gothic' symphony is one of the longest ever written, earning a mention in the *Guinness World Records*. It lasts 106 minutes and uses four soloists, two orchestras, four brass bands, an organ and as many choirs as you like. To give you some idea of the orchestral scale, the score has as many as 54 staves' worth of instruments playing together on occasion.

Mahler's Third Symphony is not far behind in the 'longest ever written' stakes, clocking in at around 95 minutes with six movements.

CHAMBER MUSIC

EINE KLEINE NACHTMUSIK, MOZART

This 'little night music' is a joyful, exuberant string ensemble work – Serenade No. 13 for Strings in G Major, to give it its proper title – and one of the most popular, and most recorded, of his compositions. Try the allegro – you'll certainly recognise it.

PIANO QUINTET IN E-FLAT MAJOR, SCHUMANN

This is a joyful piece, not a note too many or too few, with clever interweaving of string parts with the piano. A truly Romantic composition full of longing and surprising changes of mood and tempo. The second movement has an almost funereal feel, while the third has scales galore, punchy syncopation and a slower section to settle down the listener. There's a double fugue in the broad last movement, and effervescent statements combined with little legato (smooth) intermissions. This composition was dedicated to his wife, Clara. What a gift!

STRING QUARTET, OP. 64, NO. 5, IN D MAJOR, ('LARK'), HAYDN

The lark of the title can be heard in the first violin theme from the start, and for an idea of what sonata form sounds like, this first movement fits the bill perfectly. There's more of the first violin in the second movement, a minuet and trio in the third and a rip-roaring fizz of a vivace hornpipe in the fourth.

OCTET FOR STRINGS IN E-FLAT MAJOR, MENDELSSOHN

The themes of the first movement of this octet are so assured that it could almost be a finale. But there's much more to come – a rather sad and regretful little andante, followed by a scherzo with a delicate little pizzicato ending. In contrast, there's a real verve and vigour to the fourth movement. It's a work of great stature and maturity but, amazingly, Mendelssohn was only 16 when he composed it, in 1825.

MUSIC THROUGH THE AGES: PART THREE

ROMANTIC TO LATE ROMANTIC PERIOD (c. 1810–1900)

Passion, romance, drama, tempestuous self-expression, a fascination with magic, the exotic, the sensual – these were the feelings and the interests that were shaping the newly emerging art form: romanticism. Beethoven was still there, pushing forward the forms that Mozart and Haydn had perfected, as a bridge between the classical period and this new outpouring of musical passion, but now witness Gustav Mahler, Richard Wagner, Johannes Brahms, Frédéric Chopin and Franz Liszt.

These composers were still using the now established musical forms, including the symphony, the concerto, the sonata and chamber music; but key changes, richer harmonies and lyrical melodies were packing their pieces with an emotional punch.

And to complement this innovative artistic longing came important technical advances – the orchestra was getting bigger, more like the size we're used to today, not least because of improvements to the key structure of wind instruments and the invention of valves for brass instruments (making it easier to play more notes) which gave rise to the expansion of both sections.

Also, music, once the preserve of royalty and the rich, suddenly became more accessible to the general public because of the increasing numbers of concert halls.

Recommended listening

Schubert's 'Trout' Quintet in A Major strikes the perfect balance between piano and strings; the languid opening tones of the violin and the bubbling piano motifs paint pictures of a hot summer day by the river.

And for accompaniment

o The **woodwind** and **brass** sections of the orchestra expanded, the latter was given added versatility by the invention of the valve system.

o New instruments such as the **piccolo** (a half-sized flute) and the **contrabassoon** (also known as the double bassoon, and the larger cousin to the bassoon) put in an appearance. The **celeste** also appeared. It looks like a mini upright piano but has a much softer tone.

GRACE NOTE

Tchaikovsky uses the celeste for 'The Dance of the Sugar Plum Fairy' from the ballet *The Nutcracker.*

ROMANTIC RASCALS

MENDELSSOHN, FELIX (1809-47)

Unlike Schubert's family, Felix Mendelssohn's were well off – he didn't have to starve in a garret for his art – but, like Schubert, his life was cut short at an early age.

He grew up in Berlin and by the age of 13 he was already showing prodigious musical talent at the keyboard; his sister Fanny was also musically talented. It was around this time that his music teacher, Carl Friedrich Zelter, introduced him to the philosopher Goethe, and a firm friendship – and an inspiration for his music – was formed between the old man and the boy.

It is incredible to think that by the age of 16 Mendelssohn had written the overture to *A Midsummer Night's Dream* and his Octet for Strings, which is heralded for its maturity and exuberance.

Mendelssohn travelled widely through Europe in his early years, and much of his music at the time was influenced by this trip including his Symphony No. 3 in A Minor ('Scottish'), dedicated to Queen Victoria; his Symphony No. 4 in A Major ('Italian'); and his overture 'The Hebrides'.

In the summer of 1834, he accepted an invitation to take over Leipzig's Gewandhaus Orchestra, during which time he reintroduced the public to 'forgotten' works, such as Beethoven's Ninth Symphony and Bach's *Passions*. Schubert's Symphony No. 9 in C Major received its posthumous premiere there, and Mendelssohn invited the leading soloists of the day to perform. His energy seemed unbounded, devoted as he was to raising musical standards, and to establishing the role of the conductor that we see today.

He was loved and feted in England, and in 1846 his great oratorio *Elijah* premiered at the Birmingham festival. Overworked and grieving the death of his beloved sister Fanny, he died from a series of strokes in 1847. He was 38.

Recommended listening

The Piano Concerto No. 1 in G Minor, Op. 25, is unusual in that within the structure of a classical concerto there would normally be quite a long orchestral introduction before the solo instrument (the piano in this case) comes in. But in this concerto, the piano enters almost immediately with a positive eruption of chords and flowing quavers. Mendelssohn makes a powerful point of dramatic intent right at the start, which continues throughout the whole piece. A brass fanfare, fiery tempos and a pianist at full flowing stretch, this piano concerto is a powerhouse of a piece that tests the pianist's skills to the limit.

CHOPIN, FRÉDÉRICK (1810-49)

Chopin will be forever associated with the piano, and the technical challenges set by his solo compositions. He just about sums up the Romantic period: a passionate keyboard virtuoso troubled by ill health and doomed to a premature death.

He was born in Warsaw, and from an early age, showed a precocious gift for the piano, enrolling at the Warsaw Conservatory at the age of 16. Always interested in Polish culture and music, many of his compositions reflect the rhythms of his native country – his mazurkas (folk dances) are prime examples.

In 1829, he made his debut in Vienna by playing his own set of variations which were very well received; his second concert there was just as successful. He then returned to Warsaw where he fell in love with a young singer at the conservatoire. Sadly, though, the shy Chopin only admired the young lady from afar. It was while in the throes of this unrequited love that he composed his two piano concertos; the slow movement of the one in F minor was apparently inspired by his passion.

In late 1930 he embarked on a tour to Prague, Vienna, Munich and, finally, Paris – where his music was loved – but he was finding performing increasingly difficult.

Admired by many of his musical contemporaries, he was widely sought after as a piano teacher and mixed in wealthy and artistic circles. His troubled relationship with the writer George Sand, and a disastrous winter trip with her to Majorca, worsened his already ill health. These years, though, were fertile musically, writing preludes and his C-sharp Minor Scherzo.

The affair ended in 1847, and by this time, Chopin was seriously ill with consumption. His last public appearance was at a charity concert given in aid of Polish refugees. At his funeral in October 1849, Mozart's Requiem was performed, at his request.

Recommended listening

Étude Op. 10, No. 3, in E Major, later set as a two-part song 'O Lovely Spring', begins with a simple left-hand accompaniment which provides a charming basis for the lyrical melody. The piece progresses to a mini climax of strong chords, and powerful repeating themes in a (sadder) minor key, reminiscent of a sudden spring shower, just as quickly dying away to introduce the main theme once again (in the happier major key).

GRACE NOTE

Chopin's Waltz in D Flat, Op. 64, No. 1 is known as the 'Minute Waltz'. The story has it that a publisher, seeing that it was a short piece, christened it the 'Minute Waltz' (as in 'Small Waltz'). And the story does make sense as the waltz lasts around two and a half minutes. The maestro himself christened the piece 'Valse du Petit Chien' ('Little Dog Waltz') after seeing a little dog chase its tail.

SCHUMANN, ROBERT ALEXANDER (1810-56)

Love had a lot to do with Schumann's musical driving force –
another true Romantic. As a young man, he had piano lessons
with Friedrich Reich and fell passionately in love with Friedrich's
daughter, Clara, who was a brilliant pianist. However, her father
thought Schumann was a bit of a bounder and was having none
of it; it took six years of legal wrangling before they were finally
married.

Perhaps Clara's father had a point, for although Schumann
had succumbed to family pressure to study law, he abandoned
this idea eventually as he was devoting far more time to music.
He also drank heavily, and throughout his life, he showed
signs of mental instability. Their marriage was relatively happy,
though not without its strains. Clara and Robert tried hard to
be mutually supportive in their musical endeavours; Clara, the
famed pianist, and her husband, the composer. Clara continued
her concert tours as they needed the money, especially as they
went on to have a large family.

Although an injury to his hand had put paid to Schumann's
career as a performer, it didn't stop the composition of a vast
amount of piano music, songs, symphonies, chamber music and
song cycles.

Sadly, by 1853, Schumann's mental illness was worsening, and
in February 1854, he began to experience hallucinations. He was
admitted to an asylum after a failed suicide attempt, and Clara was
not allowed to see her husband again, until she was summoned to
his deathbed in 1856. It was the composer Brahms, a good friend of
the Schumanns, who regularly visited the dying man.

Recommended listening

The joyous and irrepressible Piano Quintet in E-flat Major, Op.
44, composed in 1842.

LISZT, FRANZ (1811–86)

'[He is] the incontestable incarnation
of the modern piano.'

CAMILLE SAINT-SAËNS

Like Chopin, Liszt was a master of the piano, and on hearing the brilliant violinist Niccolò Paganini play in the 1830s, he was inspired to achieve new technical heights in his own field. He wrote some cracking music, too, and was responsible for creating the genre the symphonic poem (an orchestral piece based on a work of literature or folk tale). And if this wasn't impressive enough, the enigmatic Liszt – looking pale and gaunt, his long hair flowing, charismatic expressions of agony and ecstasy flitting across his face while he was playing – proved a magnet for the ladies.

Because Liszt showed prodigious talent at the piano and in composition from an early age, his family moved from Hungary to Vienna in 1821 so that he could have lessons from the composer Carl Czerny (who was an ex-pupil of Beethoven's). Visits to Paris and a royal command performance for George IV in London confirmed Liszt's stature as a young performer.

By the time he was 16, the strain of constant touring and the death of his father forced him to re-evaluate his life and he gave up performing. He lived quietly with his mother in Paris, teaching piano, where he fell in love with one of his pupils. Refused permission to marry her, Liszt fell ill, withdrew from the world, and even considered joining a seminary.

It took the ideals of the French Revolution to raise him out of his lethargy, and during the early 1830s, he was surrounded and inspired by the leading Romantic composers of the day – Berlioz, Paganini and Chopin – being particularly influenced by the latter's style.

In 1833, he fell in love again, this time with the (married but estranged) Marie d'Agoult, who bore him three children. They lived in Switzerland and Italy, but Liszt's eventual return to the concert platforms of Europe – and the hysterical adulation his showmanship and technical piano skills received from the ladies – proved too much for their relationship and they separated in 1844.

After several years of touring and wild womanising, Liszt settled at the court in Weimar as *kapellmeister* in 1848, where he met Princess Carolyne zu Sayn-Wittgenstein. It was the Princess who persuaded him to concentrate on composing, which included the penning of his first orchestral works.

Eventually alone once more, he spent most of his final years in Rome where he took minor holy orders in 1865; not surprising then that his latter compositions were mostly sacred. He died of pneumonia in 1886, in Bayreuth, during the festival.

Apart from his fiendishly difficult piano music, Liszt is probably best remembered for his études, his Hungarian rhapsodies, his symphonic poems and his piano arrangements of other composers' works.

Recommended listening

Sonata in B Minor, written in 1854, is passionate and compelling. Even reading the score is an art, let alone playing it.

GRACE NOTE

Liszt's daughter Cosima became the second wife of German opera composer Richard Wagner, in 1870. Together, Cosima and Richard founded the great Bayreuth Festival.

WAGNER, RICHARD (1813-83)

There are generally two schools of thought when you listen to Wagner's music – he of the operatic epics – you either love it or loathe it. One thing, though, you certainly can't ignore it: *Tannhäuser*, *Lohengrin* and the massive 'Ring Cycle', a collection of the four operas *The Rhinegold*, *The Valkyrie*, *Sigfried* and *The Twilight of the Gods*, are just some of Wagner's compositions. With the 'Ring Cycle' lasting a whopping 16 hours, whoever sings in it requires a powerful set of lungs and the stamina of an ox.

But it was this extraordinary vision, this writing of compositions never seen before on such a grand, dramatic scale, and this complexity of music that led to his being regarded as one of the most controversial composers of his generation. 'One can't judge Wagner's opera *Lohengrin* after a first hearing, and I certainly don't intend hearing it a second time,' declared Gioacchino Rossini. One critic wrote, 'This din of brasses, tin pans and kettles.'

It didn't stop him, though, for this (hardly modest) master of the music marathon inaugurated a festival devoted entirely to his own work in the Bavarian town of Bayreuth, in 1826. It's still going strong today, with audiences waiting years for tickets.

Growing up in Leipzig, and surrounded by a family who loved the theatre, it's not surprising that he was already writing plays in his teens and he began his career as a chorus master in provincial theatres while writing his first opera, *Die Feen* (*The Fairies*). After a brief, unsuccessful stint in Paris, he returned to Germany in 1842 and began composing in earnest. His hard work paying off, he was appointed *kapellmeister* at Dresden.

His *Tannhäuser* opera had two premieres, firstly in Dresden in 1845, then (in an attempt to win over the people of Paris) in France in 1860 with an altered ending. The libretto (text) is quite naughty in places, and the opera's theme of sexuality versus spirituality was one that Wagner used a lot in his later works. His last opera, *Parsifal*, is 5 hours long, so if you ever go and see it, catch a good night's sleep beforehand.

Recommended listening

The overture to *Tannhäuser*. It starts slowly but there's an inexorable building up to the brass main theme, with those delicious shiver-inducing semiquavers in the strings about two and a half minutes in.

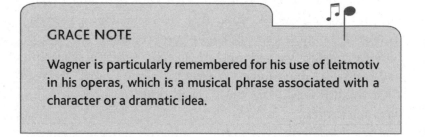

GRACE NOTE

Wagner is particularly remembered for his use of leitmotiv in his operas, which is a musical phrase associated with a character or a dramatic idea.

VERDI, GIUSEPPE (1813–1901)

Verdi is the other opera giant of this period, but unlike Wagner, it's probably safe to say that much of his music is instantly recognisable – it's certainly easier to hum some of his tunes. Even if you're not an opera buff, you'll have heard the 'Drinking Song' from *La Traviata* (*The Fallen Woman*), composed in 1853, 'The Chorus of the Hebrew Slaves' from *Nabucco*, 1842, and the music from the overture to his opera *La Forza del Destino* (*The Power of Fate*), 1862, which has been used in a Stella Artois advert.

We may not have heard many Verdi operas at all due to tragic family events. His two infant children sadly died in quick succession in 1838 and 1839, and although his first opera,

Oberto, had been produced with some success in 1839, it was while he was working against the clock on the comic opera *Un Giorno di Regno (King for a Day)* in 1840 that his wife died. The opera was a flop and Verdi came close to giving up composing for good. It was more than 50 years later when he wrote his second, and final, humorous opera, *Falstaff*, in 1893.

Having been plunged into despair on losing his family, and the failure of his opera, Verdi was eventually sent the libretto for the opera *Nabucco* and, inspired by the story, he began composing again. *Nabucco* received its first performance in 1842 and was a huge hit – giving Verdi the push that he needed. The floodgates opened and the operas flowed, including *Rigoletto, Il Trovatore (The Troubadour), La Traviata* (although that was an initial failure) and *Don Carlos*.

Verdi had a constant battle with the censors, who were always on the prowl for something that might offend public decency. 'I don't want any of those ordinary subjects which crop up by the hundred,' wrote Verdi. He had a real wrangle over *Rigoletto*, for example, the story of which – as we know it – revolves around the dissolute Duke of Mantua. However, it was based on a play by Victor Hugo, which originally depicted a womanising king of France as its principal character. This enraged the censors and so the character of the king became the duke... By the time Verdi finished it, characters' names had been altered and some scenes were cut, but the production was a triumph for everyone. (Apart, that is, from the singer who played the hunch-backed Rigoletto, who was apparently very uncomfortable with his false hump.)

Verdi is notable for putting his own dramatic mark on opera, the structure of which up until then had been quite formal. His glorious melodies were made even better by the fact that he wrote parts for particular singers, so their voices fitted the roles perfectly.

When he died of a stroke in 1901, his popularity was such that many thousands of mourners walked through Milan in honour of the great man.

Recommended listening

The overture to *La Forza del Destino* (*The Power of Fate*) is a good example of how different moods are created by different instruments, beginning with loud brass chords and followed by a tumultuous string melody, which is quietened down by a lyrical theme from the flute, and later the clarinet. Verdi's use of brass and strings together is inspiring.

BRAHMS, JOHANNES (1833-97)

There is much about Brahms' musical output that is transitional – his symphonies are in classical form but lots of his piano melodies are unashamedly Romantic in flavour. He composed for many different genres: chamber music, pieces for piano, voice and violin, and – reflecting his love of literature – more than 200 songs.

Born in Hamburg, like many of the great composers, Brahms showed musical talent from an early age and was about 15 when he gave his first piano recital.

In 1853, Brahms met Robert and Clara Schumann, who were both impressed by his talents. On hearing him play, Clara Schumann wrote in her diary:

> *'He played us sonatas, scherzos etc. of his own, all showing exuberant imagination, depth of feeling and mastery of form. Robert says there was nothing he could tell him to take away or add.'*

Brahms' devoted friendship with Clara was to last long after the death of her husband in 1856.

He held a court appointment near Hanover from 1857 to 1860 and founded a women's choir in Hamburg. Many people, though, considered his music old-fashioned and it was when he moved to Vienna that his music was more warmly received. It was his *A German Requiem* in 1868, dedicated to his late mother, that established his place in Europe as one of the great composers.

This success may have fired his creative ambition once more, and he finally completed his Symphony No. 1 in C Minor (he'd started it in 1854 and it took until 1876 for it to receive its premiere). He travelled widely over the next years, and three more symphonies were completed, as well as a violin concerto, piano trios and quintets, and many chamber and vocal works. By 1890, he had resolved to put down his pen and enjoy life, but the lure of composition was too great, and he wrote pieces for the clarinet and a song cycle.

His dear friend Clara Schumann died in 1896, and the following year, Brahms (who never married) died from liver cancer. He is buried in Vienna's central cemetery.

Recommended listening

Brahms wrote the *Variations on a Theme by Joseph Haydn* (also known as the *Saint Anthony Variations*) in 1873, composed from a piece called the *Chorale Saint Antoni* which was attributed to Hadyn (though never proved). It is a good example of Brahms' approach to orchestral writing; clear, uncluttered and the composer at his inventive best. This is the piece to begin with if you don't know his work.

TCHAIKOVSKY, PYOTR ILYICH (1840-93)

'Truly there would be a reason to go mad
were it not for music.'

Has there always been a direct correlation between suffering and musical genius? You might be forgiven for thinking so, because Tchaikovsky was another deeply unhappy composer who used his music as a salve to cope with his difficult and tortured life, including an unhappy marriage and a struggle with his sexuality.

He took piano lessons as a child, but was expected to go into the civil service, and so in 1850 was enrolled as a boarder at Saint Petersburg's School of Jurisprudence (the training ground for would-be administrators). He felt the separation from his mother very deeply and her death in 1854 was a trauma that affected him for the rest of his life.

By the age of 22, he'd had enough of his desk job and entered the music conservatoire at Saint Petersburg. He studied with Anton Rubinstein, Anton's brother Nicolai eventually offering Tchaikovsky a place in 1866 at the newly founded Moscow Conservatory to teach harmony. He began to compose in earnest – works around this time included his first symphony, his first piano concerto and, in 1875–76, the ballet *Swan Lake*.

Although his music contains many Russian influences – the themes of his second symphony, 'Little Russian', are based on Ukrainian folksongs, for example – many of his fellow composers, such as Alexander Borodin or Modest Petrovich Mussorgsky, never considered him a 'nationalist' composer, being suspicious of the Western influences that his conservatoire training brought to his compositions.

Two women in Tchaikovsky's life had a profound effect on his music. One of his conservatoire students, Antonina Milyukova, began pestering him with passionate letters. Perhaps thinking that marriage might bring an element of 'normality' to his sexual nature, and also because he was working on his great opera *Eugene Onegin* (the story of a young man who rejects a woman's love) at the time, he met her and married her in 1877. It was an immediate disaster and brought him to the brink of suicide. After only a few weeks, he fled to Saint Petersburg and never saw her again.

This emotional turmoil brought more works including his fourth symphony; his violin concerto, composed by the shores of Lake Geneva; and the completion of *Eugene Onegin*.

At about the same time, a wealthy widow named Nadezha von Meck had commissioned the composer to write some works for her; she provided him with an allowance so he was able to leave the Moscow Conservatory and compose full-time. And so began a friendship that lasted 14 years – they never met but corresponded by letter. In 1890, she abruptly ended their patronage, claiming bankruptcy (but more likely due to family pressures over her attachment to the composer).

His fame spreading, and with the '1812 Overture', the Manfred Symphony in B Minor, and his fifth symphony under his belt, he settled down in a country house near Moscow where he lived from 1892 until his death. His last major work, and his sixth symphony, dubbed 'Pathétique', was written there. Nine days after Tchaikovsky conducted its premiere in Saint Petersburg he died, aged 53, supposedly from cholera, and although suicide theories have always circulated, nothing has ever been proved.

Recommended listening

The Festival Coronation March in D Major, composed in 1883 for the coronation of Tsar Alexander III, has a stirring, almost militaristic feel to the opening, full of brass bravado and a sturdy string melody for accompaniment. A slightly more balletic feel to the melody, around 3 minutes in, provides a mood change until the processional music returns.

DVOŘÁK, ANTONÍN LEOPOLD (1841-1904)

It must have been quite something when the Czech composer Dvořák was taken under the great Brahms' wing. In 1874, Dvořák had entered an Austrian music competition held to give financial support for up-and-coming musicians. Brahms was on the jury (reluctantly, by all accounts) and was so impressed with Dvořák's music that he helped his career along. Certainly, up until then, the 33-year-old Czech was virtually unknown.

Dvořák's father was a butcher and he might have followed suit were it not that his family recognised his musical talent. He took organ, violin and piano lessons, and in 1859 graduated after two years at Prague's Organ School. The young man found a job playing the viola in a local orchestra, supplementing his income by teaching the piano. He married one of his pupils, Anna Čermáková, and they had nine children – it's a wonder he had any time for composing.

Like Tchaikovsky, Dvořák was deeply fond of his home country and often utilised folk music rhythms in his compositions – his *Slavonic Dances* composed in 1878 and 1886 are great examples. Although his early musical output was considerable – including five symphonies, string quartets, operas, vocal and piano music – the dances put him firmly on the musical map, especially as it was Brahms' own publisher who had commissioned them. Dvořák never forgot to whom he owed this recognition, and they kept in regular contact.

From then on, Dvořák's works were heard everywhere. He visited London, and was invited to write a new symphony (No. 7 in D Minor) for the Royal Philharmonic Society. In 1892, lured by the offer of a huge salary, he spent three years in New York as director of the National Conservatory of Music. Discovering America's folk heritage – and thrilled by what he heard – led to the writing of some of his greatest works, including the magnificent Ninth 'New World' Symphony, his Cello Concerto in B Minor and the lesser known String Quartet No. 12 ('American'). The third and fourth movements of the latter have something of the New World about them, and in the inner parts of the fourth movement, there's what could be described as a train moving merrily along.

Returning home in 1895, his final years were spent contentedly composing opera and chamber music, and he visited London again in the following year to conduct the premiere of his Cello Concerto. In 1897 came an emotional visit to Brahms on his deathbed; Dvořák's own death occurring in 1904.

Recommended listening

The Cello Concerto in B Minor, Op. 104. The first movement has a stately, flowing orchestral lead until the cello enters, taking up the orchestral theme and expanding it musically. The second, slow movement really sings, with beautiful interweaving themes by the cello and woodwind. The third movement is clever; it begins in march time and builds to a terrific climax, when suddenly the momentum is interrupted with a cello line that soars high over the orchestra, until the last few bars of music are left to the orchestra alone.

GRACE NOTE

Antonín Dvořák had a passion for steam trains, and once said, 'I would give all my symphonies for inventing the locomotive.'

FAURÉ, GABRIEL (1845-1924)

Fauré's musical career began on finding a harmonium in the chapel next door to the school at which his father taught. Later known as the 'master of *mélodie*', he admitted that there was very little technique to his playing in those early days but that he was very happy.

Aged only nine years old, he went to study the organ at the composer Louis Niedermeyer's music school in Paris. After Niedermeyer died in 1861, the composer Saint-Saëns took Fauré under his wing as his pupil and encouraged him to start composing; it was while he was at the school that he wrote one of his finest works, the little *Cantique de Jean Racine* (1864).

After he left the school in 1865, he held various church organist posts, but the Franco–Prussian war intervened in 1870 and he volunteered for military service. After his discharge, he returned to Paris, and was appointed assistant organist at Saint-Suplice, eventually taking over Saint-Saëns' role as choirmaster at L'Église de la Madeleine. It was while he was there that he began work on his lyrically dramatic Violin Sonata No. 1, and it was this work that caught the public's attention, its premiere a great success. In the late 1880s he began work on his requiem but it wasn't until 1900 that he considered it finished, even though it had received its first performance in 1888.

In 1896 he was appointed professor of composition at the Paris Conservatory (later becoming its director), and while there, taught an impressive array of budding composers, including the young Joseph-Maurice Ravel.

Beethoven wasn't the only composer to have been afflicted by deafness. Tragically, in his later years Fauré's hearing too was affected, the first signs of it appearing in 1902. In 1920, aged 75, Fauré resigned his position at the conservatoire to live in creative retirement. It is ironic, then, that this period not only brought him his long overdue fame, but also the writing of some of his most wonderful chamber music, including his piano trio, some sublime songs and his one string quartet.

Recommended listening

Cantique de Jean Racine. Originally scored for piano and voice, the flowing quaver triplets, which give support to the sustained main theme, provide a deceptively simple introduction to the bass voices' entry. That this recurring melody of such beauty can be captured in just three or four notes shows a startling musical maturity in a nineteen-year-old.

He wrote many beautiful songs, one of the most popular being the reflective and yearning 'Après un Rêve' ('After a Dream'). A simple but beautiful melody, its recurring triplet rhythm (three beats played within a two-beat time) is played over a left-hand foundation of chords.

These pieces provide a good sample of Fauré's musical career, and finishing with 'In Paradisum' from his requiem will round them off nicely.

SPOTLIGHT ON THE PERFORMERS

Every classical musician will tell you that to get to the top takes years of dedication, perfecting technique for hours a day. One story goes that an old lady bumped into the late jazz trumpet player Louis Armstrong: 'Excuse me, my good man,' said the lady, 'How does one get to the Albert Hall?'

With a grin, he replied, 'Practice, man, practice.'

In common with the great composers, many artistes show musical talent when very small and start their studies at an early age. But for the elite of talented youngsters, mainstream teaching is not for them – they go straight to music college for complete immersion into the world of music.

For professional artistes, it's not just their voice or their instrument that they must keep in trim – it's their person as a whole. Just like athletes, performers have to keep fit in order to be able to function at optimum level. They must warm up their bodies before a show and cool down afterwards, in the same way sportspeople do before and after a sporting event.

This is an essential part of the performer's preparation, because performing is not the only thing that they have to deal with. Many musicians have gruelling concert schedules, often spending most of the year on tour – and touring is tiring, especially as most musicians have to travel to concert venues that are at different ends of the country (or the world). Even top-flight performers such as Julian Lloyd Webber have had their touring moments – when he was in Bulgaria years ago, he found that his room was bugged and the loo didn't work.

THE VOCALISTS

HITTING THE HIGH NOTES

Whether it's performance day or not, singers need to keep their voices in trim by warming them up daily if they are to manage demanding techniques such as cadenzas and trills.

And there are many things singers have to guard against; there's always the possibility of getting a cold, for instance. Also, they must be careful to restrict their intake of cheese and milk, as dairy products can thicken the mucus in the airway, making it difficult to sing through. Central heating and air conditioning can dry the air out too much – and consequently the singer's throat.

> *'Technique is the basis of every pursuit.'*
> **JOAN SUTHERLAND**

One of the most important things that a singer must learn is breath control, as the breath fuels the voice. Listen to your breathing now – it's probably quite shallow. Unconsciously we breathe in slowly and exhale more quickly (especially when we sigh); but in order to sing long or technically difficult phrases the singer has to turn that on its head by breathing in quickly and keeping control over the amount of air exhaled. This enables a steady flow of air and produces an even singing tone. The technique is achieved with support from the diaphragm – and it takes a lot of practice.

VIVACIOUS VOCALISTS: THE LADIES

CALLAS, MARIA (1923–77)

*'I wouldn't have dared to cross swords
with Callas. I would rather have gone
six rounds with Jack Dempsey.'*

JOHN HUSTON

American-Greek soprano and singing superstar Maria Callas,
also known as 'la Divina', was famed for her revival of the
bel canto (a beautiful singing tone with great vocal technique)
operas, such as *Lucia di Lammermoor* by Gaetano Donizetti.
Her private life was every bit as fascinating as her onstage career;
her temper was as fiery as her voice was darkly sublime.

WHAT A PERFORMANCE!

The tempestuous Callas caused a scandal in 1958 when she
decided she had a sore throat and walked out after the first act
of a gala performance of Vincenzo Bellini's *Norma* at the Rome
Opera. Little did it seem to matter that the President of Italy was
in the audience.

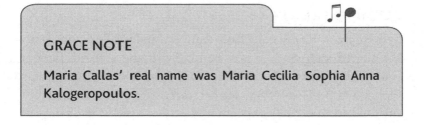

GRACE NOTE

Maria Callas' real name was Maria Cecilia Sophia Anna
Kalogeropoulos.

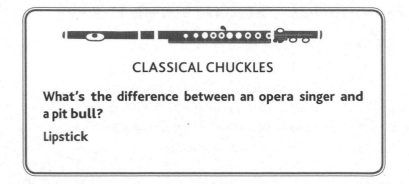

CLASSICAL CHUCKLES

What's the difference between an opera singer and a pit bull?

Lipstick

SUTHERLAND, JOAN (1926–2010)

Known as 'la Stupenda', this Australian soprano had a stupendous, agile Wagnerian voice that certainly equalled her nickname. Joan Sutherland was known as a *coloratura* soprano, which means singing lots of high notes with embellishments, trills and fast runs (the Queen of the Night solo from Mozart's *The Magic Flute* is a great example of a *coloratura* solo). Her repertoire of roles was vast, from the lighter Mozart operas right through to the big guns such as Verdi. She wasn't a great dramatic actress like Callas and sometimes her diction was criticised, but what a range of notes she could sing – her voice was considered a vocal miracle – and, unlike Callas, she was the most modest of prima donnas.

FLEMING, RENÉE (B.1959)

Lyric soprano Renée hails from America, and while at university she started singing in a jazz band. She trained at the famous Juilliard Performing Arts School, and, winning the Metropolitan Opera auditions in 1988, set her career firmly on track (she's since made over 200 appearances at the 'Met'). She sang the role of the Countess in *The Marriage of Figaro* that same year, making a triumphant debut. Her repertoire of roles and her ability to sing across a wide range of musical styles is amazing – from Tatyana in Tchaikovsky's *Eugene Onegin*, Desdemona in Verdi's *Othello*, and Marguerite in Gounod's *Faust*, to most of the Mozart soprano roles, and the title role in Franz Lehár's *The Merry Widow*. She has sung at some amazing occasions, including performances at the 2008 Olympic Games in Beijing and singing on the balcony of Buckingham Palace as part of the Queen's Diamond Jubilee Concert in 2012.

GRACE NOTE

The ultimate accolade must be Fleming's appearance on *Sesame Street*, singing an operatic aria called '1, 2, 3, 4, 5' to help children learn to count, accompanied by accordion-playing sheep and grunting pigs wearing cowboy hats.

NORMAN, JESSYE (B.1945)

If you want to hear red-hot power and a spectacularly rich, immense voice – especially in the middle register – then feast your ears on Jessye Norman. Born in Georgia, she listened to opera on the radio when she was little and started singing seriously when at university. She's particularly known for her Wagnerian repertoire but has excelled in roles such as Verdi's *Aida*, as Dido in *Dido and Aeneas* by Purcell and the title role in Bizet's *Carmen*.

BAKER, JANET (B.1933)

A mezzo-soprano noted for her interpretations of British music, Benjamin Britten's particularly, Janet Baker found fame the hard way. She moved from Yorkshire to London in the 1950s to take singing lessons, while working at a bank to make ends meet. At 23, she came second in the Kathleen Ferrier Memorial competition and in 1956 she joined Glyndebourne's chorus. She made her Covent Garden debut in 1966, singing the role of Hermia in Britten's *A Midsummer Night's Dream*. She excelled in works by Handel and Bach, and in 1982, she gave her farewell performance as Orfeo in Gluck's *Orfeo ed Euridice* (although she continued to give lieder recitals for another seven years).

TE KANAWA, KIRI (B.1944)

New Zealand-born Kiri te Kanawa is renowned for her mellow voice, and for her interpretations of Mozart and Strauss. As well as opera and oratorio, Kiri has produced a series of popular recordings by George Gershwin, Cole Porter and Irving Berlin. In 2010 she appeared as Nellie Melba in *Downton Abbey*.

WHAT A PERFORMANCE!

Kanawa was watched by a global audience of 750 million viewers when she sang 'Let the Bright Seraphim' from *Samson* by Handel at the wedding of Charles, Prince of Wales, and Diana, Princess of Wales, in 1981. Admired for her glamour and sense of style, her rainbow dress with a ruffled collar coupled with a bright blue pillbox hat was as bright as her singing.

Check out these performers too...

DE LOS ÁNGELES, VICTORIA (1923-2005)

Spanish lyric soprano, always more at home on the concert platform, commands an impressive middle range of notes.

GHEORGHIU, ANGELA (B.1965)

Romanian soprano, especially renowned for her performances of Puccini.

CABALLÉ, MONTSERRAT (B.1933)

A Spanish soprano with an extraordinary bel canto repertoire, and the most awe-inspiring breath control – also famous for singing with Freddie Mercury.

HORNE, MARILYN (B.1934)

Born in Pennsylvania, she is a mezzo-soprano probably best known for her interpretations of works by Rossini.

VON OTTER, ANNE-SOFIE (B.1955)

When she's not making records with Elvis Costello, Swedish von Otter is widely known for her varied repertoire, including lieder, oratorio and rock songs.

VIVACIOUS VOCALISTS: THE GENTLEMEN

CARUSO, ENRICO (1873–1921)

Probably one of the most famous Italian opera tenors of the early twentieth century, Enrico Caruso was certainly not quite the handsome romantic figure as portrayed by Mario Lanza, being a bit on the short side and a little chubby. But what a singer! Even though he was a lyrical tenor, his voice had a richness to it reminiscent of a baritone (see Glossary), and in his later years, he always avoided singing a high C. He made his first recording in 1902, in a hotel room in Milan, and was the first recording star in history to sell more than a million records.

WHAT A PERFORMANCE!

Caruso was involved in a scandal in November 1906, when he was charged with an indecent act committed in the monkey house of New York's Central Park Zoo. Police accused him of pinching the bottom of a woman; Caruso claimed it was a monkey that did the bottom-pinching.

DOMINGO, PLÁCIDO (B.1941)

A tenor, a conductor, an humanitarian and one third of the Three Tenors, Spanish-born Domingo had auditioned as a baritone for the Mexican National Opera in 1959. However, when he was asked to sing something in the tenor range, it became clear that this was his voice category. He made his debut as Alfredo in Verdi's *La Traviata* in 1961. As of 2013, he had sung more than 3,000 performances of 144 roles (more than any other tenor) and has conducted any number of performances. Now, aged 74, he shows no sign of slowing down: 'When I rest, I rust,' he has said.

PAVAROTTI, LUCIANO (1935-2007)

The big man from Modena with the big voice (and the hanky) to match, and another third of the Three Tenors. He gained his first musical experience by singing in the city's opera chorus, of which his father (a baker) was also a member. As a teenager, he was part of this choir which travelled to sing at the International Eisteddfod in Llangollen, and which won first prize. He made his debut as Rudolfo in *La Bohème* in 1961.

He was in the right place at the right time when Joan Sutherland was looking for a tenor taller than she was to go on a tour of Australia with her. He got the job, and he credited Sutherland for his great breathing technique that stood him in such good stead throughout his phenomenal career. He gained a worldwide reputation on the concert platform where his blisteringly beautiful top register earned him the soubriquet 'The King of the High Cs'.

GRACE NOTE

Pavarotti sang his last performance, one of his most renowned solos, 'Nessun Dorma' from Puccini's opera *Turandot* at the opening of the 2006 Winter Olympics.

CARRERAS, JOSÉ (B.1946)

The remaining member of the Three Tenors, Spanish José Carreras has had more than most to contend with during his long career, being diagnosed with leukaemia in 1987 during the shooting of a production of *La Bohème* in Paris. Following gruelling treatment, though, he resumed his career.

He set out originally to study chemistry, but left university to concentrate on singing. His opera debut came in 1970, taking the role of Flavio in Bellini's *Norma*. Spanish soprano Montserrat Caballé was so taken with Carreras' performance in *Norma* that she invited him to appear opposite her in Donizetti's *Lucrezia Borgia* as Gennaro. He has occasionally branched out from opera, recording *West Side Story* with Kiri te Kanawa and *South Pacific*. His voice has been described as being 'richly coloured and sumptuously resonant'.

BOCELLI, ANDREA (B.1958)

This Italian opera tenor learned the piano, saxophone and flute from an early age but had his first vocal success when he won a singing competition in 1970. His lucky break came when he recorded a demo tape of 'Miserere' for the Italian rock singer Zucchero Fornaciari – who'd held auditions to find a suitable tenor – to send to Pavarotti in the hope that they could sing it together. After hearing Bocelli on tape, Pavarotti urged the rock star to use Bocelli instead. Although Zucchero eventually persuaded Pavarotti to record the song with him, Bocelli sang 'Miserere' with the rock star on his 1993 European tour.

Bocelli has gone on to duet with Sarah Brightman in 'Time to Say Goodbye' and collaborate with Celine Dion, Jennifer Lopez and Plácido Domingo. He made his debut in a major operatic role in 1998, as Rodolfo in a production of *La Bohème*.

MELCHIOR, LAURITZ (1890–1973)

If you like Wagner, then Lauritz Melchior was the leading Wagnerian tenor of the 1920s, 1930s and 1940s. Like Domingo, he started his career as a baritone until someone at the Royal Danish Opera had a feeling that Melchior was 'a tenor with the lid on'. He soon took the lid off with the title role in *Tannhäuser*.

GIGLI, BENIAMINO (1890–1957)

Italian again, and seen by many as Caruso's successor, although he preferred to be judged on his own merits. They called him 'Caruso Secondo' which he (not surprisingly) disliked – he preferred 'Gigli Primo'. Certainly, his voice was described as 'honey' and was closer to a lyric voice than Caruso's. He made his La Scala debut in 1918 as Faust.

BOE, ALFIE (B.1973)

Many agree he has a dreamlike voice, this light tenor from Fleetwood, Lancashire. He started off in musical theatre, notably *Les Misérables*, but he's pretty accomplished at Handel and Verdi, and was recently awarded a fellowship from the Royal College of Music.

FISCHER-DIESKAU, DIETRICH (1925–2012)

A German lyric baritone who was probably the finest singer of lieder of the twentieth century. His technique was such that he had absolute control over his voice; he had an excellent sense of rhythm and his sensitive colouring and interpretation of songs left the audience knowing that they had heard a quite extraordinary artiste. Although he's remembered principally for his brilliant interpretation of Schubert's songs (he recorded more than 400 of them), he also sang many operatic roles, having made his debut at the Municipal Opera in Berlin in 1948. Benjamin Britten personally asked him to sing in the premiere of the *War Requiem* in 1962 in the rebuilt Coventry Cathedral.

ALLEN, THOMAS (B.1944)

Thomas Allen is County Durham's – and some say the world's – finest lyrical baritone. He was going to be a doctor but a place at the Royal College of Music put paid to that. He joined the Welsh National Opera in 1969 and made his Covent Garden debut as Donald in Benjamin Britten's *Billy Budd*. Since then, he's added countless roles to his repertoire, 50 of them with the Royal Opera. His powerful stage presence is matched by a warm, fruity voice with tremendous range and power.

WHAT A PERFORMANCE!

He may be at home with the big Wagnerian roles and German lieder, but Allen's lightness of voice was shown to great advantage during the Proms in 2009 when he sang songs from MGM film musicals. He also performed a great updated version (complete with notebook!) of Gilbert and Sullivan's song 'I've Got a Little List' from *The Mikado* during the Proms in 2004.

TERFEL, BRYN (B.1965)

Welsh big boy Bryn Terfel is blessed with an equally big (and spine-tingling) bass-baritone voice to match. He graduated from the Guildhall School of Music and Drama in 1989 (winning the Kathleen Ferrier Memorial prize) and made his opera debut with the Welsh National Opera in 1990 in *Così fan Tutte*. Coincidentally, his Royal Opera House debut in *Don Giovanni*, in 1992, saw him perform alongside Thomas Allen in the title role. He's another opera singer who has made popular music recordings, including the songs of Richard Rodgers and Oscar Hammerstein II.

WHITE, WILLARD (B.1946)

Listen to baritone Paul Robeson singing 'Ol' Man River', and you're halfway to hearing the smooth tones of Jamaican bass-baritone Willard White. He has a sensational, dark, melted-chocolatey deep voice, and his version of 'Ol' Man River' is something else. He discovered singing by listening to Nat King Cole on the radio. He studied with Maria Callas at New York's Juilliard School and made his first professional appearance in 1974 in *La Bohème*. Willard was the second black actor to play *Othello*, in Trevor Nunn's 1990 Royal Shakespeare Company production.

THE STRINGS

STRINGED IRRITANTS

'God save me from a bad neighbour and a beginner on the fiddle.'

ITALIAN PROVERB

If you're a violin player, there's always the chance that a string will snap and ping you right on the chin. Then there's 'fiddler's neck' – a red skin rash underneath the chin, just below the angle of the jaw where the violin is held. Back, neck and shoulder ache… leathery fingertips… and tendonitis is always a threat. And what about the lighting in the orchestra pit? The violinist certainly suffers for their craft.

Then, of course, there are the difficulties of travelling with an instrument. 'Two first class tickets, please – one for me and one for the double bass.'

GRACE NOTE

Researchers at Massachusetts Institute of Technology have been studying what gives the Stradivarius violins their unique sound. They found that the more elongated the f-shaped sound holes on each side of the violin are, the more sound they can produce. Studies suggest that the gradual elongation of the sound holes happened accidentally over time, as the violin-makers tried to replicate an original blueprint.

BOWERS AND SCRAPERS

PAGANINI, NICCOLÒ (1782–1840)

It wasn't only his 24 Caprices for Solo Violin, so beloved of many composers, that the Italian showman Paganini was famous for – he was also one of the most remarkable violinists the world has ever known. There was the whiff of something extraordinary about the way this man could play the violin – some said his talent was the result of a pact with the devil – and he certainly looked the part with his long flowing hair, cadaverous face, and the facial expressions he pulled when he played. Pizzicatos with both hands, double-stopping and glissandos (see Glossary), and octave trills – you name it, he could play it. The public adored him and he toured extensively, giving recitals all over the world. Sadly, though, by 1834, Paganini had pretty much exhausted himself, and he retired to Parma for the rest of his days.

CLASSICAL CHUCKLES

Belgian-born John Joseph Merlin invented roller skates. In 1759, he skated into a ballroom playing a violin to unveil his new set of wheels but, unfortunately, he didn't know how to stop and crashed into a full-length mirror, breaking his violin.

HEIFETZ, JASCHA (1901–87)

This Lithuanian-born musician is deemed one of the best violinists of the twentieth century. He began playing the violin from the age of two, his father having picked up on his talent early, and made his first public appearance when he was eight years old. This marked the beginning of a career lasting more than 60 years. He appeared at Carnegie Hall in New York when he was 16, making one of the most sensational debuts the country has ever witnessed. Would-be violinists aspire to his intonation, his ability to play the violin with a precision that few have matched since, and the beautiful tone he produced.

KREISLER, FRITZ (1875–1962)

Austrian violinist Fritz Kreisler's life was quite extraordinary: he entered the Vienna Conservatory at the age of only seven, made his American debut at 13 and the great Edward Elgar composed a violin concerto for him. He was known for his eloquent interpretations of Beethoven, and for the lovely tone his playing produced. He also used to play little pieces at his concerts which he had composed himself but which were in the style of earlier composers such as Couperin and Vivaldi. They went down rather well until he owned up to having written them, at which point the critics (who didn't like being fooled) complained loudly.

MENUHIN, YEHUDI (1916-99)

A child prodigy, Menuhin was born in New York and was playing to adoring audiences by the time he was seven. He made his first recording in 1931, but it was his recordings of Elgar's Violin Concerto in B Minor, with Elgar conducting, and his interpretation of Beethoven's Violin Concerto in D Major that caught the public's attention. During World War Two he performed for the Allied soldiers, and for the survivors of the Belsen concentration camp.

Not hidebound by classical music, he explored other genres, with Stéphane Grappelli and Ravi Shankar. Concerned for the musical wellbeing of the next generation of musicians, he founded the Yehudi Menuhin School in 1963 – Nigel Kennedy was a pupil there.

KENNEDY, NIGEL (B.1956)

Aston Villa, *The Four Seasons*, Poland... these all add up to just one name: the inimitable violinist Nigel Kennedy. Or just Kennedy. A protégé of Menuhin, he studied at the Menuhin School, then at the Juilliard School in New York. He made an appearance with the jazz violinist Stéphane Grappelli when he was only 16, and his recording debut of Elgar's Violin Concerto in 1984 marked him as one to watch. But of course the composition he's most famous for is Vivaldi's *The Four Seasons*, to which he brings a very special emotional intensity – and it's one of the highest-selling classical records ever.

He's known these days not only for his accent and his hairdo, but also for his love of other musical forms, jazz in particular.

(Not all critics have taken to his jazz-like cadenzas in some of the classical works he's played.) He now divides his time between Worcestershire (where his son lives) and Krakow (where he plays jazz), his second wife being Polish.

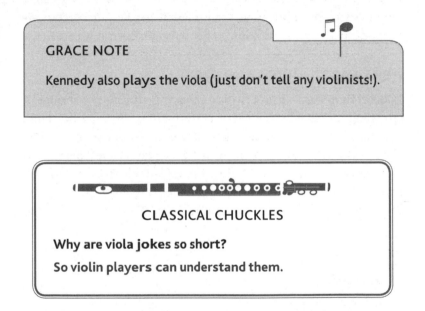

GRACE NOTE

Kennedy also plays the viola (just don't tell any violinists!).

CLASSICAL CHUCKLES

Why are viola jokes so short?
So violin players can understand them.

OISTRAKH, DAVID (1908–74)

This renowned Russian violinist was known particularly for his interpretations of Dmitri Shostakovich's works, with whom he was friendly. His son, David, also became a violinist and they performed various works together, including Bach's Double Violin Concerto.

MUTTER, ANNE-SOPHIE (B.1963)

A German violinist who began playing at five years old, she made her professional debut at the 1978 Lucerne Festival. A year later she played with Herbert von Karajan and the Berlin Philharmonic Orchestra. Hailed as one of the world's greatest violin virtuosos of our time, she is known for her interpretations of modern works in addition to her strong classical repertoire.

BENEDETTI, NICOLA (B.1987)

Nicola Benedetti is not just a great violinist, she brings a sparkling personality to every performance. Born in Scotland, she studied at the Menuhin School, and at 16, she won the BBC Young Musician of the Year award. Since then, she's performed to royalty, worked with conductors and orchestras worldwide and won numerous awards, including Best Female Artist at the 2012 and 2013 *Classical Brit Awards*.

GRACE NOTE

Benedetti has had the opportunity to play two Stradivarius violins, firstly the 1723 Earl Spencer, then the 1717 Gariel.

GRACE NOTE

In 2007, as part of a social experiment, the world famous violinist Joshua Bell pretended to be a street violinist in Union Station, Washington, and almost everyone ignored him. The violin he used on the street was worth around $3.5 million.

CASALS, PABLO (1876–1973)

Bach lovers will know that Pablo Casals is remembered principally for his recordings of the Bach Cello Suites and his flawless technique. He studied piano, violin and organ. However, when a group of travelling clowns came to his Spanish village, and Casals saw one of them playing a crude version of a cello, he immediately knew that this was the instrument he wanted to play. As a teenager, he came across a manuscript of some of the Bach suites and spent more than ten years practising them before he would consider performing them in public – his recording of the suites still remains one of the greatest.

He studied composition at Madrid Royal Conservatory, and by the end of the 1890s, he had performed in front of Queen Victoria. He made many recordings of solo work, chamber and orchestral music, and the depth and sound of his playing as well as his exemplary phrasing remain unequalled. He is remembered, too, for his conducting and, away from the concert platform, his tireless stance against dictatorship and oppression, being fiercely opposed to the dictator Francisco Franco's regime.

ROSTROPOVICH, MSTISLAV (1927-2007)

There were two cellists who dominated the musical world in the twentieth century, Pablo Casals was one and the other was Mstislav Rostropovich. In addition to being a great cellist, he was known for his support of Russian dissidents, giving shelter to Alexander Solzhenitsyn. This angered the Soviet authorities, who limited his performances and stripped him of his citizenship in 1978. He settled in America and did not return to Russia until 1990 (when Mikhail Gorbachev restored his citizenship). Like Casals, he was also a conductor, and was music director of the National Symphony Orchestra in Washington for 17 years.

Where Casals had concentrated on particular works, Rostropovich's repertoire was wide-ranging. Many well-known composers wrote works for him, including Shostakovich, Messiaen and Britten, and his technique and warm tone were also a perfect match for works by Tchaikovsky and Haydn.

DU PRÉ, JACQUELINE (1945-87)

Jacqueline du Pré's brilliant career is made all the more poignant because it was so brief, and you cannot listen to her exquisite version of Elgar's Cello Concerto without an overwhelming sense of sadness of a life cut short. Watching her performances, it's hard to know where the person ends and the cello begins because they seemed so at one.

As a child, she is said to have heard the cello on the radio and from that moment on all she wanted was to become a cellist. At 16, du Pré made her debut at the Wigmore Hall in London, and in 1996, at 21, she studied in Russia with Mstislav Rostropovich. She married pianist and conductor Daniel Barenboim in 1967, and performed for little more than ten years before being diagnosed with multiple sclerosis in 1973. She died in 1987, aged 42.

YO-YO MA (B.1955)

This French-born American-Chinese cellist was not only a child prodigy, he has also played with Yehudi Menuhin in front of royalty and American presidents, and has won 15 Grammy awards – like Renée Fleming, he has had the honour of playing on *Sesame Street*! Added to this, he is known to be a pleasure to work with and has an ebullient personality (incidentally yo means 'friendship' in Chinese), and gives master classes to nurture the next generation of cellists.

He was five when he played his first concert, and although he went to the Juilliard School in New York, unusually he then enrolled at Harvard University to broaden his horizons. He, like Casals, is widely known for his interpretation of Bach's Cello Suites, as well as for his collaboration with pianist Emanuel Ax to play chamber music.

Yo-Yo Ma is artistic director of the Silk Road Project, which he founded in 1998 to bring together different cultures through music, in particular those along the ancient Silk Road, which separates China from Europe and Asia.

FOURNIER, PIERRE (1906–86)

French-born Fournier, known for his formidable bowing technique, originally learned the piano but took up the cello as a child as a result of a mild case of polio – his weakened legs made it difficult for him to use the piano pedals. After graduating from the Paris Conservatory, he made his debut a year later in 1925, and was hailed as the 'cellist of the future'. He worked with the great conductors, such as Herbert von Karajan, and had a considerable repertoire: Bach and Beethoven, in particular, but also modern composers, such as Claude Debussy and Francis Poulenc.

TORTELIER, PAUL (1914-90)

Another Frenchman, whose first performances were to accompany silent films in cinemas in Paris. A graduate of the Paris Conservatory, he first played with the Monte-Carlo Philharmonic Orchestra, then as solo cellist with the Boston Symphony Orchestra in 1939. He was a music professor at the Paris Conservatory from 1956 to 1969, but he became well known as a soloist after playing in a performance of *Don Quixote*, under conductor Thomas Beecham, in 1947.

His elegant, passionate playing, in addition to his career as a composer, makes him interesting listening.

THE PIANISTS

KEYBOARD CONSIDERATIONS

Before sitting down at the piano, it's advisable to carry out a few stretches to warm up the body and to release tension in the neck and arms. Make sure your posture is good and the seat is adjusted to the correct height.

A typical warm-up might well include arpeggios (see Glossary), scales, an exercise or two and a favourite piece – and all most likely done in a freezing cold rehearsal room early in the morning. Without warming up properly, there's always the potential for RSI (repetitive strain injury), particularly to the wrist. And what's more, pianists constantly face the eternal struggle of how to keep their fingers warm; the challenge of having a repertoire of many pieces fresh at their fingertips every day... Plus every piano in every concert hall will 'play' differently, unless, of course, you can travel with your own (and it has been done). Make that one economy ticket for you, and the rest of first class for the piano!

PIANO PERFECTIONISTS

'My whole trick is to keep the tune well
out in front. If I play Tchaikovsky, I play
his melodies and skip his spiritual struggle.'

LIBERACE

ASHKENAZY, VLADIMIR (B.1937)

Pianist-conductor Ashkenazy – hardly ever seen in performance without wearing his trademark white polo-necked jumper – began playing the piano when he was six. Unlike some of his Russian musical contemporaries, who chose to stay in Russia during the years of repressive rule, he eventually took Icelandic citizenship (his wife's nationality) in 1972, having left the Soviet Union permanently in 1963.

After studying at the Moscow Conservatory, he rose to prominence when he shared first prize at the International Tchaikovsky Competition with pianist John Ogdon. During his career, he has recorded extensively – including Mozart, Rachmaninoff, Bach, Schumann, Prokofiev – and he is known particularly for his interpretation of the piano works of Chopin. It was a natural progression that he should branch out into conducting, leading many famous orchestras, including the Royal Philharmonic Orchestra, and serving as conductor laureate at the Sydney Symphony Orchestra.

LANG LANG (B.1982)

One of the things that inspired Lang Lang to play the piano was when he heard Liszt played (by Tom) in the *Tom and Jerry* episode 'The Cat Concerto'! But cartoons aside, it has been well documented that the Chinese pianist had a difficult childhood, his father being a strict disciplinarian.

Away from home, studying to enter the Beijing Central Conservatory of Music, the nine-year-old hit an all-time low, not least because Lang Lang's piano teacher told him that he had no talent, and when his father heard about it, he angrily told his son that he should kill himself.

However, one day, Lang Lang was persuaded to sit down and play some Mozart. From that moment on, he knew he was born to play, and one of the greatest pianists of the modern era was on his way again. He played the complete Chopin Études at 13 years of age; he was appointed as a last-minute soloist, replacing Andre Watts, to play a Tchaikovsky concerto with the Chicago Symphony Orchestra at 17; he has won 56 Grammys; he has collaborated with a number of world-famous artists; and his concerts sell out wherever he plays – and he's still only in his thirties!

RICHTER, SVIATOSLAV (1915–97)

> *'Give lessons? Good heavens, no!*
> *If anything I ought to take a few myself.'*

Perhaps he made the remark because he was largely self-taught, and for an artist of such skill it's remarkable that Richter didn't begin formal training until he was in his early twenties. By the time he did, he'd already had a stint as a rehearsal pianist with Odessa Opera – where his excellent sight-reading skills were most useful – and he gave his first recital at 19.

He went to the Moscow Conservatory and, while there, made his debut playing Prokofiev's Sonata No. 6, the composer being so impressed that he gave the young pianist his Sonata No. 7 to premiere in 1942. He was known for his effortless technical mastery and beautiful tone, brought out to the full in his repertoire of not only his beloved Prokofiev, but also Bach, Schubert, Liszt and Chopin.

He was an enigmatic, private man who disliked making records – most of them are live recordings – and who preferred to play by the light of a small lamp, to let the music speak for itself.

GRACE NOTE

Richter's friend Marlene Dietrich wrote in her autobiography of an incident when a woman sadly died during one of his performances. She pondered, 'What an enviable fate, to die while Richter is playing.'

BRENDEL, ALFRED (B.1931)

When Austrian Alfred Brendel retired from the concert hall in 2008, he did so typically of the man who had entertained concert audiences with his technical brilliance on the piano for the best part of 60 years – without fuss and bother. But retiring at the peak of his playing powers meant more time for Brendel to focus on his other career, that of writing poetry, music articles and essays, and also lecturing and teaching.

He studied at Graz Conservatory in Austria, but apart from this formal period of study, Brendel was largely self-taught. At 17, he gave his first public recital, 'The Fugue in Piano Literature', which included a performance of his own sonata. His career progressed step by step, and in the 1960s he became the first pianist ever to record the entire piano works of Beethoven. The pairing of Brendel with Beethoven was inspired; as Brendel's performance of Beethoven's Piano Concerto No. 5, 'Emperor', shows, they were a no-nonsense duo full of lyrical power and passion.

RUBINSTEIN, ARTHUR (1887–1982)

Born in Poland, Arthur Rubinstein was arguably one of the finest pianists of the twentieth century; however, there was considerable competition for the title in his early years, the composer Rachmaninoff for one. His beautifully bright tone and his joy of music, and playing perfectly, matched the brio of his life. His *joie de vivre* obviously served him well, as he performed for more than 80 years, dying peacefully at the great age of 95.

ARGERICH, MARTHA (B.1941)

Argerich is Argentinian, and perhaps not so widely known as some of the other performers featured in this book, as she has appeared on stage little since the 1980s, concentrating less on solo work and more on chamber music ensembles. A pity, because at 24 she won the International Chopin Piano Competition in Warsaw, debuting in the States the same year. Her playing is outstanding and unpredictable, and her repertoire includes everything from Domenico Scarlatti to Béla Bartòk.

BISS, JONATHAN (B.1980)

American Jonathan Biss was surrounded by music from his birth – his parents both violinists, and his grandmother a cellist. He made his New York debut in 2000 and his Carnegie Hall debut in 2011. Biss is unusual in that he tends to immerse himself and explore one composer for a while. Over a period of what will eventually be nine years, he will have recorded all Beethoven's Piano Sonatas (due to be completed in 2020). He has also explored Schumann's musical legacy, too. Not just a great pianist, his musical curiosity is fascinating.

ZIMERMAN, KRYSTIAN (B.1956)

This Polish pianist is a firehouse of talent – direct, impassioned and with a technical clarity that is awe-inspiring. He won first prize as a 19-year-old at the 1975 Warsaw Chopin Competition and has since toured the world, performing with top orchestras and conductors. He prefers live performances, and in recent years has halted a performance because of an audience member filming him. Quite within his rights – apart from disturbing the rest of the audience – as filming a performance of any kind without permission is theft.

THE BLOWERS

WIND WOES AND BRASS BURDENS

Playing wind instruments requires really high breath pressure, which can result in *laryngoceles*, the air sacs near the larynx sometimes appearing as bulges on the outside of the neck. The musician's embouchure, or mouth position, is so important that any tooth loss or gum disease can throw everything out. Then there's 'English horn player's thumb' – tendonitis again.

THE BLOWERS

GALWAY, JAMES (B.1939)

The man who is as twinkly as his golden flute playing, James Galway began his musical career by learning folk tunes, and he freely admits to playing all the time as a child, even on his way to school. He studied at the Paris Conservatory, under the flautist Gaston Crunelle, and then joined a number of orchestras, such as Sadler's Wells, Covent Garden Opera, the London Symphony Orchestra and the Royal Philharmonic. From 1969 to 1975 he was principal flautist of the Berlin Philharmonic, but left to pursue a solo career.

What is so notable about his playing – apart, that is, from a tone praised for being exquisite in its purity and a flawless technique – is that he has crossed the boundaries between classical and popular music without losing anything in translation: from Bach and Beethoven to 'Annie's Song' and Howard Shore's *The Lord of the Rings* soundtrack. His biography reads like a Who's Who of modern times – he's performed for royalty, popes and presidents, and has worked with musicians from Henry Mancini to Andrea Bocelli, from Ray Charles to Elton John. Despite international acclaim, Galway has always kept in touch with his roots, too, with collaborations closer to home including those with fellow Irishmen, The Chieftains, in the 1980s.

BRYMER, JACK (1915-2003)

Another mostly self-taught musician, Brymer started to learn the clarinet from a very early age, attracted to the sound by listening to his father who played the instrument in his spare time. Playing in various groups and bands gave him the invaluable experience of learning other genres, such as jazz and light music, as well as classical.

He trained to be a schoolteacher and during the war served in the RAF as a physical training instructor. Back to teaching after the end of the hostilities, word of Brymer's clarinet playing reached the mighty Thomas Beecham, who was looking for a clarinettist for the Royal Philharmonic Orchestra. Brymer auditioned and got the job, remaining with the orchestra for 16 years. Periods with the BBC Symphony Orchestra and the London Symphony Orchestra, and a professorship at the Royal Academy meant that his sublime tone and vibrato became instantly recognisable worldwide.

BLISS, JULIAN (B.1989)

Not only a great clarinettist but he designs them, too. Jazz, classical, swing, you name it – he is one of the music industry's brightest stars. Born in St Albans, Bliss started playing at four years old, went off to America to study and now plays all over the world with the great orchestras. He launched his own septet in 2012, both at Wigmore Hall and Ronnie Scott's Jazz Club, being equally at home playing Mozart or Benny Goodman. Watch Bliss play – it takes fiendishly good technique and mastery over an instrument to make it look so effortless.

BRAIN, DENNIS (1921–57)

If you're of a certain generation and can remember the duo Flanders and Swann with their French horn song, chances are you may have heard the real thing – the immortal third movement of Mozart's Horn Concerto No. 4 in E Flat – played by Dennis Brain. For just as Jack Brymer had popularised the clarinet as a solo instrument, Dennis Brain was responsible for putting the French horn firmly on the musical map. Sadly, his extraordinary technique and strength of personality was cut short in a car accident in 1957 – a cruel blow for the world of music and for the public. Luckily, he has left behind (among other records) the definitive recordings of all Mozart's Horn Concertos, with Herbert von Karajan and the Philharmonia Orchestra.

> ### GRACE NOTE
>
> Dennis Brain once played Concerto for Hosepipe and Strings by Leopold Mozart (Wolfgang's dad) at a Gerard Hoffnung music festival in the 1950s. Just the third rondo movement, if you're wondering.

OVERCOMING DIFFICULTIES

Over the years, both composers and performers have had to overcome many personal challenges: Beethoven's deafness; Robert Schumann's battle with mental illness, the injury to his hand and his short-sightedness; Frederick Delius who was blinded and paralysed by syphilis; and Bruckner who would probably now be diagnosed as having OCD (obsessive–compulsive disorder).

But as frustrating and heart-rending as it must have been for them all, it didn't stop them – in fact, some of the most beautiful classical music has been composed or played under extreme pressure and the most difficult of circumstances.

It is widely known that **ROBERT SCHUMANN** (1810–56) suffered an injury to his hand. However, there are some differences of opinion as to how it occurred. Was it the mechanical device he used to strengthen his fingers? Others put forward the theory that it was a side effect of mercury poisoning after being treated for syphilis. Whatever the theories, it sadly put paid to his career as a pianist.

LÉON GOOSSENS (1897–1988) was one of the twentieth century's greatest oboists, and came from a musical family – his father was a violinist, his brother was a conductor and his sisters were the harpists Marie and Sidonie Goossens. He was principal oboist of the Royal Philharmonic Orchestra and undertook worldwide tours. Many British composers wrote works for him, including Benjamin Britten and Edward Elgar.

One of the most difficult things for the would-be oboe player to learn was the correct use of the facial muscles and the lip-shaping – the embouchure – in order to produce the correct pitch, dynamics and tone.

It was, therefore, a tragedy – and an ironic one at that – when Léon Goossens was involved in a head-on collision in 1962 that resulted in serious injuries to his lips, face and teeth. In an interview, he explained that as well as sustaining life-threatening injuries to his body the steering wheel's horn ring broke off and lashed across his mouth. It required 150 stitches and left the muscle under his bottom lip completely numb. It threatened his career but, undeterred, he developed a new technique of bunching up the muscles at each side of his mouth in order to be able to play again and, by 1966, he did.

PHYLLIS SELLICK (1911–2007) and **CYRIL SMITH** (1909–74) enjoyed a long and happy relationship as a married couple, fellow pianists and duettists. They met at the Royal College of Music and married in 1937.

Although the war curtailed their professional performances somewhat, they toured with the Entertainments National Service Association (ENSA) as a duo, and after the war, they had a family.

All was well until 1956, when Cyril suffered thrombosis which resulted in him losing the use of his left arm. Undaunted, they set about playing duets for three hands, being so successful that composers such as Malcolm Arnold wrote pieces especially for them.

Born in Lancashire, **KATHLEEN FERRIER** (1912–53) had the most bewitching, rich contralto (see Glossary) voice and it is a tragedy that her life was cut short by cancer when she was only 41 years old. She'd originally studied the piano, but left school at 14 to find work at the General Post Office in Blackburn. It was when she won a local music contest as a singer that her career began. In 1942 she met conductor Malcolm Sargent, who was deeply impressed by her voice, and in 1946, she made her stage debut at Glyndbourne in Benjamin Britten's *The Rape of Lucretia*. She was well known on the concert platform, singing all the great oratorios, and went on tours worldwide. Her version of 'Blow the Wind Southerly' is known as the definitive version.

In February 1953, Kathleen must have been in great pain when she sang for the last time as Orfeo in Gluck's *Orpheus and Eurydice* at Covent Garden. Knowing she was dying, her performance and her aria, 'Che Farò?' ('What is Life?') was hailed by her fellow singers as extraordinarily moving. During the second performance her hipbone shattered, weakened by the disease and radiation treatment. Despite the agony, she was determined that the audience should not know, and continued until the end of the performance before being taken to hospital. It was her last public appearance.

EVELYN GLENNIE (b.1965) is a Scottish percussionist known the world over for her innovative playing – and she's the first person in history to create and sustain a full-time career as a solo percussionist. Evelyn has made over 30 solo recordings, has won three Grammy Awards and was recently named 2015 Laureate of the Polar Music Prize (the musical equivalent of the Nobel Prize). She's also remarkable in that she has been profoundly deaf since the age of 12. In an interview with the BBC, she said, 'There's no such thing as total deafness. If the body can feel, that is a form of hearing. Sound is vibration.' She uses her body as a 'huge ear'.

ITZHAK PERLMAN (b.1945), the Israeli-American violinist, is one of the finest violinists of the twentieth and twenty-first centuries – his performance of Beethoven's Violin Concerto in D Major sings. But Perlman always performs sitting down, as he contracted polio when he was four years old, and although he made a good recovery, he has always walked with the aid of crutches. He is a global ambassador for the elimination of polio.

RUSSELL WATSON (b.1966) is the tenor with the golden voice who rose from the factory-shop floor to the international concert stage, and who has sung for royalty and world leaders. He is as at home with ballads as with operatic arias, and his albums have sold in their thousands. What you might not have known is that he has had more to deal with than most, undergoing two operations in 2006 and 2007 to remove a brain tumour. Back singing again since 2008, his career has gone from strength to strength.

Cellist **JULIAN LLOYD WEBBER** (b.1951) greatly saddened the classical music world in 2014 when he announced his retirement from performing due to a neck injury. The Royal College of Music graduate made his debut in 1972 at the Queen Elizabeth Hall and is regarded as one of the finest cellists of his generation. His injury – a herniated disc in his neck – has left him with reduced power in his bowing arm. However, music will still fill his life, as he is now principal of Birmingham Conservatoire.

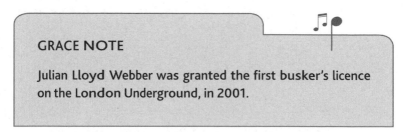

GRACE NOTE

Julian Lloyd Webber was granted the first busker's licence on the London Underground, in 2001.

MUSIC, MUSIC, MUSIC: DEXTERITY AND POWER

The intricate precision of a Bach toccata, the perfect form of a Beethoven sonata or the inspiring changes of mood in 'The Planets' are just some of the musical compositions to whet the appetite. Here are some further suggestions for your classical music delectation.

TOCCATAS

TOCCATA, WIDOR

It's commonly known as Widor's 'Toccata' but, actually, the theme we know is from the fifth movement of Widor's Fifth Symphony for Organ in F Minor. It is a glorious riot of syncopated semiquavers underneath long pedal notes and will leave you breathless – especially the huge, sustained loud chords at the end. This piece is often heard reverberating around a church at a wedding – many brides have featured it, including royal ones: Princess Margaret to Antony Armstrong-Jones in 1960; Anne, Princess Royal, to Mark Phillips in 1973; and Sophie, Countess of Wessex, to Prince Edward, Earl of Wessex in 1999.

TOCCATA AND FUGUE IN D MINOR, BWV 565, BACH

This piece is played on the organ and begins very dramatically – it's the twirling opening motif that is so recognisable (and has been played in many a horror movie). This is the perfect piece to listen to if you're new to Bach. Incidentally, the BWV stands for Bach-Werke-Verzeichnis (Bach Works Catalogue), which is the numbering system used to identify his works.

GRACE NOTE

Johann Sebastian Bach's rigid adherence to the old forms of fugue and polyphony earned him the nickname 'the old wig' by his sons – to his face, we'll never know.

SONATAS

PIANO SONATA NO. 14 IN C-SHARP MINOR ('MOONLIGHT'), BEETHOVEN

Along with his piano solo 'Für Elise', the 'Moonlight' sonata is one of Beethoven's most recognisable tunes – at least the first movement is. Written in 1802 and dedicated to his pupil Giulietta Guicciardi, the slow dreamy start is in sharp contrast to the bright scherzo second movement and the agitato drama of the third movement.

PIANO SONATA NO. 20 IN A MAJOR, SCHUBERT

Full of strength and lyrical melodies, this sonata is one of three that Schubert wrote in the last year of his life in 1828. It is in four movements; the first, an allegro, begins with strong triplet arpeggios and accompanying chords, followed by lyrical melodies. The second, an andantino, moves to a slow and wistful minor key but has an unexpected outburst of fast scales and an almost improvisatory feel in the middle section. The third movement is a playful three-beats-in-a-bar scherzo that lightens the mood and sets the scene for the more majestic rondo, which is the final movement. This is Schubert at his most powerfully impressive.

SUITES

'THE PLANETS', HOLST

Holst began this orchestral suite in 1914, and it consists of seven movements – each one named after a planet – all of which are enduringly popular. With its dramatic repetitive string motif,

Mars is a terrifying vision of war. Jupiter, with its strong brass and percussion influence, is the bringer of jollity. Its second, more serious theme was adapted by Holst in 1921 as the tune set to a poem by Cecil Spring Rice. Today we know the words of this poem as the hymn 'I Vow to Thee, My Country'.

CELLO SUITE NO. 1 IN G MAJOR, BWV 1007, BACH

Not the most obvious choice, but it is a composition that should be near the top of everyone's classical music list. Bach wrote a series of six suites for cello and the first movement from this first suite, the prelude, is probably the most frequently performed and used in films. What makes these suites so special is that the solo cello is unaccompanied. The first movement of this G Major suite begins with sweeping arpeggios that rise and fall and the momentum builds and builds. Knowing that one instrument can hold an audience's attention for nearly twenty minutes (the whole suite comprises six movements) is an indication of Bach's consummate skill as a composer, and the skill and dexterity of the performer.

UNDER THE BATON

THE CONDUCTORS

THE CRAFT OF CONDUCTING

What do conductors actually do? At its simplest, the conductor is there to beat time in order to keep the orchestra together, to guide the changes of tempo, and to control the dynamics and the sound. They also cue the instruments to come in at the right place.

Their theory and technical knowledge must be tip-top, and keeping track of where the orchestra is in the music is a huge challenge as an orchestral score can be many staves deep, especially during sections when the majority of the orchestra is playing together. Look closely, though, and it is clear that some conductors know the composition off by heart.

BEAT THAT!

When it comes to technique, it's not just a case of a conductor waving their arms about – there are definite patterns to a conductor's beat (although looking at some of them in action, it would be easy to miss this!). According to how many beats in a bar there are, the first beat of a bar is the downbeat, and the last beat of the bar is the upbeat.

The right hand is commonly used to convey the beat, the left hand for cueing the musical entrances, the dynamics and the expression; the hand slowly raised, palm upward, indicates a crescendo, the palm down, slowly lowered, signals a decrescendo. The end of a beat or phrase is usually shown by the fingers being closed up, or with a flick of the wrist. However, each conductor has their own semaphore that the orchestra members learn to interpret.

Body language and eye contact with the orchestra, and the soloist if it's a concerto, also play a huge part in the conductor's role in bringing the music to life.

GRACE NOTE

Georg Solti was unhappily known by orchestra members as the 'Screaming Skull' because of his autocratic style and bald head.

MUSIC FROM THE HEART

The technicalities are really only one part of a conductor's role. Additionally, they are regarded as the conduit through which the composer's work can be shown to its best advantage. As the interpreter of the work, the conductor has to have a real vision of the piece, and to do this, they must find out what makes the composer tick. Indeed, many conductors are known for their interpretations of the works of one particular composer.

How a composition is interpreted can vary hugely from one conductor to another – some like to stick to every nuance of a composer's original idea, some will visualise the score very differently. It can be a fascinating exercise to choose a piece of music – a symphony or a concerto, perhaps – and listen to two or even three versions of the same piece but with a different orchestra and conductor. You'll notice that each one will be different.

A QUICK TIMEKEEPING HISTORY

Conductors as we know them today haven't always been around – they're a late nineteenth-century creation which evolved over time to accommodate the growing size of the orchestra.

There has always been some rudimentary form of timekeeping, and in the seventeenth century it was rather fashionable to beat time with a large stick – which sadly cost the baroque composer Jean-Baptiste Lully his life. He struck his foot with his conducting staff during a performance, and infection and subsequent gangrene set in. He refused to have his leg amputated, and so that was the end of Lully. The trend for using a baton (see Glossary) became common practice around the early 1800s – a good deal safer! The first conductor who used one regularly was Louis Spohr (1784–1859).

In the baroque era a member of the ensemble would keep everyone together in time by conducting with their violin bow when they weren't playing – or the harpsichord player, acting as the continuo, would conduct from the keyboard. Even today, smaller chamber music ensembles, quartets and quintets will have no conductor save a group member (often the violinist) who will use eye contact or incline his head to keep time and bring everyone in. The members of an ensemble who rehearse and perform together constantly will instinctively feel for each other's playing (and the same for an orchestra with a long-term conductor).

We know that Beethoven conducted some of his works and most of the nineteenth century's most famous composers were also conductors, such as Wagner, Mendelssohn and Hector Berlioz.

But the twentieth and twenty-first centuries have brought forth many renowned 'giants of the podium', some conductors staying with orchestras for many years. So who are they, these technical colossi, these charismatic interpreters of music? Here are just a few of many.

MAGNIFICENT MAESTRI

TOSCANINI, ARTURO (1867–1957)

Italian Toscanini is known as the 'conductor's conductor' and the man who made the orchestra 'talk' with his precise, brilliant intensity, his striving for perfection (with the temper to go with it) and his photographic musical memory. He single-handedly put the modern orchestra on the map and was an incomparable conductor of Italian opera.

BEECHAM, THOMAS (1879–1961)

This English conductor founded the London Philharmonic Orchestra (together with Malcolm Sargent) and the Royal Philharmonic Orchestra. It is a pity that he is remembered more for his witty put-downs than his charismatic performances on the podium and his charming interpretations of the works of Mozart.

GRACE NOTE

Thomas Beecham's grandfather, also Thomas, founded the Beecham's Pills laxative factory in St Helens in Lancashire.

VON KARAJAN, HERBERT (1908-89)

Born in Austria, von Karajan was the principal conductor of the Berlin Philharmonic Orchestra for 35 years, and is widely known for producing the most beautiful, brilliant sound from an orchestra, as well as for his interpretations of Anton Bruckner and Wagner.

RATTLE, SIMON (B.1955)

Currently conductor of the Berlin Philharmonic Orchestra, Liverpool-born Rattle is set to join the London Symphony Orchestra as its musical director. He is well known for his dynamic style and versatility of repertoire, steering his 'musical family' to greater heights.

FURTWÄNGLER, WILHELM (1886-1954)

A German conductor widely regarded as one of the most inspired of the twentieth century (and the most controversial, opting to conduct in Nazi Germany in World War Two). He was noted for the personal, intense interpretations and depth of feeling he gave to pieces of music.

ABBADO, CLAUDIO (1933-2014)

Conducting at La Scala, the Metropolitan Opera and the Berlin Philharmonic, the Italian was noted for his warm interpretations of the Romantic composers, the Italian opera and works by modern composers. He was a shy man of few words, his favourite being 'listen'.

GRACE NOTE

What do you think conductor Colin Davis liked to do when he'd put away his baton for the evening? Well, light up a pipe of tobacco for a start. But he also liked to knit, having been taught by his sisters when he was small. It brought him relaxation away from the concert platform – and some thick jumpers to wear in draughty rehearsal halls, too, no doubt.

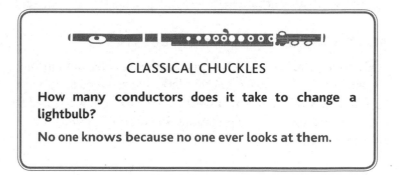

CLASSICAL CHUCKLES

How many conductors does it take to change a lightbulb?

No one knows because no one ever looks at them.

THE ORCHESTRA

> *'There are two golden rules for an orchestra:
> start together and finish together. The public
> doesn't give a damn what goes on in between.'*

THOMAS BEECHAM

THE SYMPHONY ORCHESTRA

THE BASICS

o The ancient Greek word *orchestra* meant the circular space in front of the stage reserved for performers. But gradually the word came to mean a group of musicians who played together in the said space.

o There are usually between 80 and 100 players in a modern orchestra.

o The orchestra is divided up into four sections: strings, woodwind, brass and percussion, and there is a principal player for each section.

STRING SECTION

The string section has the majority of players in a modern orchestra – around 60. Generally, there are:

o 16 (first and second) violins

o 14 violas

o 14 cellos

o Ten double bass

The violins are divided up into first and second; the first violins usually play the tune, and the second violins, the harmony (see Glossary).

The principal player of the first violins is called the **leader of the orchestra**, and is second in command to the conductor.

Strings snippets

o The violin first made an appearance in the mid 1500s, with the evolution of the symphony and the string quartet in the eighteenth century establishing its continued valuable position in classical music.

o The violin, which has four strings, is made up of 80 separate parts, with pine or spruce being used for the front (or soundboard), and a hardwood such as maple used for the back.

o The viola is the alto of the string section and is pitched a fifth below the violin. It is mainly played as a lower musical line underneath the violins, although it can be played as a solo instrument, for example in Hector Berlioz's symphony *Harold in Italy*, which has a viola obbligato (an important solo instrumental part).

o The cello's proper name is 'violincello' but is always referred to in its abbreviated form. It is tuned one octave below the viola. At about four feet long, you're unlikely to be able to tuck it under your chin, and that's why it's played with the body of the cello between the player's legs.

o The double bass is the big boy of the strings, measuring about six feet from top to toe, although, surprisingly, there's no standard size. Its strings (gut or steel) are overwound to make it more manageable to play, and they are tuned to E, A, D and G; those of five strings to B, E, A, D and G.

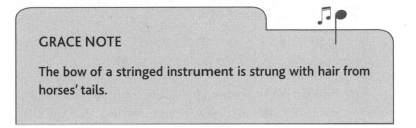

GRACE NOTE

The bow of a stringed instrument is strung with hair from horses' tails.

CLASSICAL CHUCKLES

The definition of a true gentleman: one who can play the viola, but won't.

WOODWIND SECTION

There's a variety of sizes in this section, from the tiny piccolo to the gigantic contrabassoon. The entire group is made up as follows:

- Three flutes (doubling with piccolo where necessary)

- Three oboes

- Three clarinets (E-flat bassoon, but also bass clarinet, when needed)

- Three bassoons (including contrabassoon, when needed)

Words about woodwind

o   For a start, nowadays, not all the instruments of this section are made of wood, but the name still sticks.

o   Early woodwind instruments made a bit of a racket and it was because of the need for a better sound that the flute evolved.

o   The flute was a difficult instrument to play, until German flautist Theobald Böehm came along in the 1830s and sorted out the fingering system, which included making larger holes.

o   The piccolo is pitched an octave higher than the flute – listen out for it in Nikolai Rimsky-Korsakov's *Scheherazade*.

o   The principal instrument of the woodwind section, the oboe, is a double reed instrument, and produces sound when two pieces of cane fastened together vibrate.

o   The single reed clarinet was invented at the beginning of the eighteenth century. The B-flat size is most frequently used in the orchestra.

o   The lowest-sounding member of the woodwind family is the bassoon. If you laid it out (it's usually folded in half) it would be about nine feet long.

o   The saxophone, invented by Adolphe Sax in 1840, is less commonly used in the orchestra, but is drafted in for use in specific pieces such as Maurice Ravel's *Boléro*.

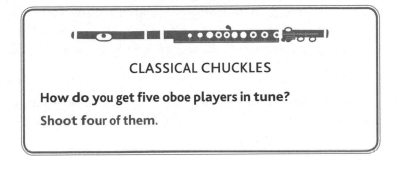

CLASSICAL CHUCKLES

How do you get five oboe players in tune?

Shoot four of them.

BRASS SECTION

Again, different sizes of the same family of instruments are used, depending on the piece being played:

o Three trumpets

o Four French horns (could be more)

o Three trombones

o One tuba

A bit on brass

o The French horn has 18 feet of tubing, wound round with a bell shape at the end. It's played to great effect in Prokofiev's *Peter and the Wolf.*

o The three-valve trumpet is the smallest member of the brass section, but instead of blowing through a reed, as wind instrumentalists do, the trumpet player vibrates his lips against the mouthpiece to produce sound.

o The tube length of a trombone is around nine feet. The trombone's pitch is in the same range as the cello and the bassoon, and the note is changed by moving the slide up and down.

o There's usually only one tuba in the orchestra, providing a musical anchor to the rest of the brass section. It takes a great deal of puff to play one.

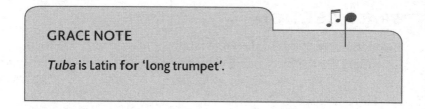

GRACE NOTE

Tuba is Latin for 'long trumpet'.

PERCUSSION SECTION

This is quite a large family because there are lots of instruments that can be shaken, hit, scraped or vibrated. Generally, though, the section comprises:

- Timpani, also called kettledrums

- Xylophone

- Cymbals

- Triangle

- Snare drum

- Bass drum

- Tambourine

- Maracas

- Bongos

- Gongs

- Chimes

- Celesta

- Piano, also known more formally as pianoforte

Percussion pointers

'The typewriting machine, when played with expression, is no more annoying than the piano when played by a sister or near relation.'

OSCAR WILDE

o Timpani are very large and usually played in pairs; the drums' pitch is altered by stretching or loosening the drumheads, which are attached to a foot pedal.

o Xylophone means 'wood sound'. It has wooden bars (which are struck with different kinds of mallet) at the bottom of which are metal resonators where the sound vibrates.

o Maracas are traditionally made from dried gourd shells containing loose seeds. Interestingly, one is often pitched higher than the other by using different seeds or beans, or differing amounts.

o The celesta looks like a tiny piano and sounds a bit like a glockenspiel as it has a lovely bell-like sound.

o The piano was invented around 1700 by Italian instrument maker Bartolomeo Cristofori. It has 88 black and white keys which lift unseen hammers that strike the strings when played. The hammer rebounds but the strings continue to vibrate until the pianist releases the key to stop the vibration. Due to it having strings and hammers, the piano can be classed as both a stringed and a percussion instrument. Unlike the plucked harpsichord, it is possible to produce loud and soft sounds on a piano – the literal translation of the piano's full name, pianoforte, is 'soft–loud'. No other solo instrument responds so well to the player's touch, and with such a range of sound and expression.

Peculiar percussion

o You probably would never have thought that a typewriter might be added to the percussion ranks but, in 1950, American composer Leroy Anderson composed 'The Typewriter', a short piece for typewriter and orchestra. Four years later he wrote 'Sandpaper Ballet' for orchestra and three grades of sandpaper.

o And while on the subject of sound effects... Erik Satie, the French composer who died in 1925, is probably best known for his set of piano compositions, *The Gymnopédies*, but he wrote a fun ballet called *Parade* – a collaboration between Satie, the writer Jean Cocteau and Picasso, which was composed for Diaghilev's Ballets Russes. The story is set in a fairground and the orchestration includes various sound effects, such as a typewriter, a foghorn, milk bottles, pistols and sirens. You could say that Picasso came out of it the best, though. He fell for one of Diaghilev's Russian dancers, Olga Khokhlova, who became his first wife.

o The percussion orchestration for Igor Stravinsky's orchestral work *The Rite of Spring* (1913) includes the triangle, the tambourine, the guiro*, two antique cymbals, cymbals, the bass drum, and the tam-tam (a large metal gong).

*A guiro is an instrument shaped like a hollowed-out gourd, with notches. It's played by rubbing a stick over the notches, and is often used in Latin American music.

THE RISE OF THE ORCHESTRA

The first 'orchestras' could hardly be termed so, as they were really just small groups of musicians who provided music for festivals or holidays. The modern orchestra originated in sixteenth-century Italy from the instrumental groups provided to accompany entertainment and dancing at court and in noble households.

Gradually, though, especially with the emergence of theatre and opera in the seventeenth century (which had arisen from these royal entertainments), these groups of instruments were combined with other sections such as woodwind and brass. Timpani put in an appearance too; Lully and Bach are both known to have composed for the instrument. Also during this period, the violin displaced the viol.

By the eighteenth century, composers were assembling musicians together specifically to play, the strings taking on a more important role as the harpsichord's continuo use fell out of fashion. Flutes, oboes and bassoons were all now regular members of the orchestra.

Technical advances in the mid 1800s helped the orchestra no end – the invention of valves for brass in 1815 made the brass section more flexible and improvements to the woodwinds' keys structure meant more woodwind instruments could join the orchestra, and it was easier for all the instruments to play in tune with each other.

By the end of the 1800s, orchestras were huge to accommodate the colossal productions by composers such as Mahler and Wagner, but after World War One, austerity led to the composition of smaller works for smaller orchestras.

And the trend has continued, with smaller groups such as the Academy of St Martin in the Fields, The Bach Players and the Academy of Ancient Music continuing to flourish. These smaller ensembles take us back to the musical styles of the past

– the Academy of Ancient Music, for example, plays baroque-era music on period instruments. Ensemble music, it seems, has come full circle.

CHAMBER ORCHESTRA

A chamber orchestra means exactly that – a small group of musicians that could fit, in years past, into a small room in a house or a palace. Originally musicians would meet together to play in homes for private celebrations, perhaps, or just for the pleasure of getting together to play.

GRACE NOTE

The largest orchestra ever assembled was by Sacramento Youth Symphony Artistic Director Michael Neumann in October 2014, when he conducted a symphony of 1,000 players. Neumann's image was projected on to a big screen so the players had a good view of his conducting.

A QUICK TUNE UP OF ORCHESTRAS...

ROYAL CONCERTGEBOUW ORCHESTRA, AMSTERDAM

This orchestra comes out tops in many concert goers' opinion, and with good reason. Founded in 1888, for years this orchestra has had a fearsome reputation for getting right under the skin of composers' works, and the sound they make is powerful and extraordinary – especially when it comes to Mahler and Bruckner. And it says something that in their long history, the orchestra has had only six conductors, including Bernard Haitink. Once they get there, they stay. The present incumbent, Mariss Jansons, who began conducting the orchestra in 2004, will leave in 2016, his successor being Italian conductor Daniele Gatti.

The orchestra gives around 40 concerts throughout the world each year, and was granted the title 'Royal' on its hundredth anniversary in 1988.

BERLIN PHILHARMONIC

Rebellious lot, those German musicians! In March 1882, a group of ensemble players directed by Benjamin Bilse were discontented with the conditions they played in and refused to sign a new contract with him. Instead, they set up their own, named The Former Bilse Ensemble; they had high hopes but it was hard to make ends meet. In 1882, with Ludwig von Brenner at the helm, the orchestra was renamed the Philharmonisches Orchester and embarked on its first tour, and it never looked back.

Hans von Bülow took over as chief conductor in 1887, and since then the orchestra has been managed by a stream of distinguished conductors – Herbert von Karajan, Claudio Abbado and Simon Rattle – earning the orchestra the reputation of being one of the best in the world.

Classical music enthusiasts agree that Simon Rattle's conducting has nurtured in the Berlin Philharmonic all the velvety sweetness for which its players are legendary.

LONDON SYMPHONY ORCHESTRA

In 2017, Simon Rattle will be leaving the Berlin Philharmonic Orchestra, where he's been since 2002, to return to his home country and, after some anticipation, lead the London Symphony Orchestra.

The LSO was formed in 1904, when 50 members of the Queen's Hall Orchestra (the original venue for the Promenade concerts) rebelled against Henry Wood's insistence that no deputies be sent to rehearsal. (It was quite common for an orchestra member to send in a replacement or 'dep' musician to play at the concert if he or she had received a more lucrative offer to play elsewhere.)

The orchestra has had many distinguished conductors over the years, including Edward Elgar conducting the world premiere of his *Pomp and Circumstance March No. 3* in 1905. John Barbirolli made his debut with the orchestra in 1927 and since then conductors have included André Previn, Pierre Boulez and Michael Tilson Thomas.

The orchestra is also very much involved in education, with its Discovery programme for schools, and concerts for families, so children can enjoy classical music – there are even storytelling concerts for the under fives.

VIENNA PHILHARMONIC

Until 1842, Vienna had no professional concert orchestra, and any symphonic works were played by ensembles specially put together for the occasion. In May of that year, the orchestra of the Gesellschaft der Musikfreunde (Society of the Friends of Music) and the court orchestra joined forces with the court opera orchestra for the premiere of Beethoven's Ninth Symphony.

Even today, only a musician who plays in the Vienna State Opera Orchestra can become a member of the Vienna Philharmonic. The orchestra has been led by some of the world's best-known conductors, such as Hans Richter, Felix Weingartner, Bruno Walter, Claudio Abbado and Daniel Barenboim.

ROYAL LIVERPOOL PHILHARMONIC ORCHESTRA

This orchestra is the UK's oldest, its origins going back to the 1830s when a group of amateur musicians met together and formed the Liverpool Philharmonic Society, and in 1844 the orchestra performed its first symphonies. It acquired the title 'Royal' in 1957 and now performs around 60 concerts each season, and has been host to world premieres of works by Michael Nyman, John Taverner and Karl Jenkins. In addition to its extensive programme working with schools, it records under its own record label, RLPO Live.

CHICAGO SYMPHONY ORCHESTRA

Founded in 1891, this orchestra celebrates its one-hundred-and-twenty-fifth anniversary in 2016. It's one of America's Big Five orchestras, the others being:

o New York Philharmonic

o Boston Symphony Orchestra

o Philadelphia Orchestra

o Cleveland Orchestra

The CSO plays a vast repertoire, from baroque to contemporary music, and its music director is the Italian conductor Riccardo Muti.

ODD ORCHESTRAS

o Until recently, five musicians who called themselves the Spaghetti Western Orchestra toured the world playing the tunes of Ennio Morricone. Sadly, they no longer tour so there's no more opportunity to hear them play 'The Good, the Bad and the Ugly' on instruments including asthma inhalers, rubber gloves, mandolins and pipes.

o The Vegetable Orchestra of Vienna was founded in 1998, and is known for playing music on fresh vegetables, such as carrot recorders, cucumberphones and leek violins.

o Musicians from the Royal Philharmonic Orchestra gave a recital in Cadogan Hall in London in 2011 to more than 100 varieties of different plants to see if music would help them grow (it was a rather clever idea to promote the gardening section of a well-known TV shopping channel). Benjamin Pope, the conductor, said that the audience was one of the most fragrant they'd ever had. Mozart's music is said to stimulate the brain, so they were hoping that his Symphony No. 40 in G Minor might trigger plant growth. The results were inconclusive.

THE CHOIRS

LEADING A CHOIR

Conducting a choir is a bit like being a plate spinner – you have to keep lots of them spinning all at once, making sure the ones you set going first don't fall off. As an example, say the repertoire consists of five pieces. Each member of the choir has to learn the piece thoroughly – that is to be pitch-, note- and interpretation-perfect with the rest of the choir by the time of the concert. At the first rehearsal, the choir goes through the notes for pieces A and B – sopranos, altos, tenors and basses – line by line. Then everyone sings it all together. It's hard work. They then reprise A and B at the second rehearsal, while starting work on piece C, and later piece D, then piece E, and so on.

But in the midst of the usual panic that the concert's not going to be ready in time, there's a sea of smiling, hardworking singers who practise diligently every week, and the concert is a success.

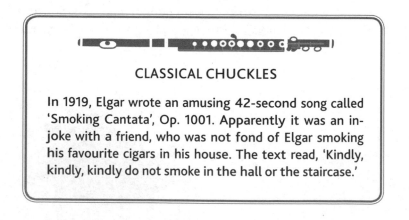

CLASSICAL CHUCKLES

In 1919, Elgar wrote an amusing 42-second song called 'Smoking Cantata', Op. 1001. Apparently it was an in-joke with a friend, who was not fond of Elgar smoking his favourite cigars in his house. The text read, 'Kindly, kindly, kindly do not smoke in the hall or the staircase.'

SCORE? CHECK. PENCIL? CHECK. VOICE? AHEM...

Up and down the country, any day of the week, groups of people get together to sing in amateur choirs – it's choir practice night. And although church, barber-shop, and ladies' choirs and choral societies have been going for years, there's one man who has been single-handedly responsible for raising the profile of UK choirs and getting those who would never have dreamed of standing up in front of an audience to do exactly that – Gareth Malone.

GARETH MALONE (B.1975)

From the moment his first series, *The Choir*, hit our television screens, Gareth's enthusiasm, expertise and optimism have put a song in many people's hearts. He has rounded up posties, pub regulars, council workers, supermarket staff, the rescue services and military wives and has introduced them to singing. Everywhere he has been he has left a trail of happy people, especially as in some cases the newly recruited choristers weren't sure of their singing abilities. The rehearsals were initially a triumph of enthusiasm over expertise, but he has brought the musical best out of everyone he has been associated with.

Bullied at school because he wanted to sing, Malone had the last laugh by storming ahead musically and graduating from the Royal Academy of Music in 2005. It all began when a production company was looking for someone to front a show about singing in schools and they appointed Malone for the job. Now, as a result of his work, he's made any number of television series and is an OBE.

ALL TOGETHER NOW – FROM THE TOP

Some of these choirs were established before Gareth was even a twinkle in his father's eye...

LUTON GIRLS CHOIR

This was one of the most popular ensembles of the 1960s and 70s, singing popular songs such as 'Count Your Blessings' on the radio, in the recording studio and abroad. Formed by agricultural agent Arthur Davis in the 1940s, in order to revive what he saw as the dying art of choral singing, the choir quickly became a household name and raised more than £100,000 for charity during its performing years.

There were strict admission rules: the singers had to live within five miles of Luton Town Hall, they had to resign from the choir at 23 years of age (or when they got married) and each member paid a choir sub of 4d weekly. None of the singers was professional, so it was straight home from work and out to choir practice. The choir was disbanded in 1977 after the death of Arthur Davies the year before.

GRACE NOTE

Such was Luton Girls Choir's fame, they sang as part of a celebrity gala variety radio programme, in June 1947, to celebrate Queen Mary's eightieth birthday; and at the Royal Command Performance the following year.

VIENNA BOYS' CHOIR

This choir of boy trebles and altos has a long and illustrious history as the choir to the Viennese courts of the Middle Ages, and which over the years has worked with one or two composers you may have heard of – Mozart, Salieri and Schubert. Until 1918, the choir sang exclusively for the imperial court but after this time, the boys' choir was established as a private institution, becoming the Wiener Sängerknaben (Vienna Boys' Choir). The boys' imperial military uniform (which included a dagger!) was replaced by the familiar blue and white sailor suit.

Today, there are around 100 choirboys between the ages of 10 and 14, divided into different touring choirs – and they sing a vast range of music, from lieder and the specially arranged waltzes and polkas of Johann Strauss and Franz Lehár, to contemporary music. Interestingly, they still fulfil their part in the tradition as imperial musicians, singing Sunday Mass at Vienna's Imperial Chapel – where they can be heard, but not seen.

TREORCHY MALE CHOIR

If you want to hear great singing then head off to Wales, the land of song, and in particular, to the Rhondda Valley, where they've been turning out cracking singers for more than 100 years.

The Treorchy Male Choir started life as the Treorky Male Choir in 1883, developing into an Eisteddfod winning choir and performing in front of Queen Victoria at Windsor Castle in 1895. It's had its ups and downs, not least through the Great Depression and two world wars, but after the original choir bowed out in 1897, the choir was reformed in 1946 and has become a national institution, with regular successes at the Eisteddfod Welsh musical festival, television appearances, radio broadcasts, albums and worldwide tours.

MONTEVERDI CHOIR

This is the brainchild of conductor John Eliot Gardiner who founded the choir in 1964, along with the English Baroque Soloists in 1975 and the orchestra Révolutionnaire et Romantique in 1989. Remarkably, in the year 2000, the choir performed all of Bach's 198 cantatas in more than 60 European churches to mark the two-hundred-and-fiftieth anniversary of the composer's death in 1750. Many of the choristers have gone on to solo careers, and Eliot Gardiner has cherished and nurtured all three groups, which he calls his 'extended musical family'.

THE SIXTEEN

Not strictly just a 'choral choir' but a combination of choir and period-instrument orchestra formed by a group of 16 friends in 1979, and founded by English conductor Harry Christophers. The group is big with Renaissance and baroque music but it also features twentieth- and twenty-first-century music. They've toured the world and made some impressive recordings.

BBC SINGERS

The BBC singers – the professional chamber choir of the BBC – has been around for more than 80 years. Its first performance, as the Wireless Chorus, was of Mendelssohn's *Elijah*. Over the years, the choir has premiered works by composers such as Benjamin Britten and Michael Tippett. Former members include the tenor Peter Pears and Harry Christophers (conductor of The Sixteen).

The choir sang through the war years, despite having to move from its Maida Vale base, and became a stalwart of the Third Programme after the war. The BBC Singers was established in 1989 and the choir continues to be in great demand today, in concert and on the radio. You'll usually be able to catch the BBC Singers on the Proms.

THE TALLIS SCHOLARS

Another Renaissance group, the Scholars, was established in 1973 by its director and conductor Peter Phillips. The Scholars sing the music of composers such as Giovanni Pierluigi da Palestrina, Thomas Tallis (of course) and William Byrd, but also modern works such as 'Sainte-Chapelle' by Eric Whitacre. Particularly impressive is their rendition of songs such as *Missa Gloria Tibi Trinitas* by John Taverner (*c.*1490–1545) – The Scholars' voices reach the rafters effortlessly, belying the fact that this work is notoriously difficult to sing.

GRACE NOTE

The Three Choirs Festival – a week-long programme of choral and orchestral concerts, music recitals and talks – rotates each summer between the Cathedrals of Hereford, Gloucester and Worcester. Local composers Elgar and Vaughan Williams have been closely associated with the festival, which celebrated its three-hundredth year in 2015.

MUSIC THROUGH THE AGES: PART FOUR

THE TWENTIETH CENTURY

In the early part of the twentieth century, there were still many Romantic composers around but they were in the final throes. The modern world was at war, struggling to come to terms with the uproar of conflict. And there was conflict musically, too. Should new composers continue to adopt the previous musical shapes and structures that had stood the test of time, or strike out with new and exciting forms? The answer is that there were composers of both kinds.

On the one hand, think of the pastoral qualities of Vaughan Williams' music – his folk song 'Linden Lea', for example, or his *Fantasia on a Theme by Thomas Tallis* for string orchestra – or Elgar's lyrically expressive melodies. Compare these to the complex, atonal music – atonal meaning a piece of music that doesn't have a tonal centre, so one almost without a sense of musical or harmonic direction, and with lots of chromatic passages – of Arnold Schoenberg. This atonal musical quality led to his devising what is known as 'serial' composition, in which all 12 notes of the chromatic scale have an equal importance (also known as Schoenberg's 12-tone technique).

Recommended listening

Schoenberg's increasing use of atonality is evident in his Five Pieces for Orchestra, composed in 1909. Audiences then were so unused to this freedom of sound that they were left baffled by its seeming chaos.

Maurice Duruflé's Requiem has recognisable elements of Gregorian chant in this moving work.

And for accompaniment

The orchestra and its instruments is very much a traditional body, but with the twentieth century came technical innovation – electronic music, a fascination to mix old and new genres and a desire to push musical boundaries.

DIVERSITY DAREDEVILS

ELGAR, EDWARD WILLIAM (1857-1934)

> *'Worcestershire was everything to him... From walking, driving and bicycling there was very little of the county he did not know.'*
>
> **CARICE ELGAR BLAKE**

Who wouldn't want to write wonderful music with the Malvern Hills for inspiration? It is little wonder that Edward Elgar became, for many, one of the most important English composers since Henry Purcell in the 1600s – and that's a long time to wait. His impressive body of work included *Enigma Variations*, *The*

Dream of Gerontius, his well-known Cello Concerto in E Minor and, of course, the *Pomp and Circumstance Marches*.

Elgar was born in Broadheath, Worcestershire. His father tuned pianos and had a music shop in Worcester, but despite being surrounded by music, Elgar was mostly self-taught musically, as far as composition and harmony were concerned, but he did have piano and violin lessons. On leaving school he started work in a solicitor's office but left after only a year to start a career as a musician, taking on anything he could, from church organist, to giving violin lessons, to becoming bandmaster at the Worcester County Pauper and Lunatic Asylum.

He'd already started composing, but his early years were a struggle: 'My prospects are about as hopeless as ever,' he wrote to a friend in 1884. He needed help.

In 1886 he married a pupil, Caroline Alice Roberts. Her staunchly Anglican family was horrified – not only was he considered to be lower class, he was a Roman Catholic to boot. However, with the marriage came the vital musical helpmate and friend he needed. Alice made it her life's aim to do everything she could to support him while he composed. They had one daughter, Carice (a contraction of his wife's names).

Slowly but surely, through works such as his overture 'Froissart', which was a commission from the Worcester Festival, and his cantatas *King Olaf* and *Caractacus*, his fame as a composer began to spread. It was his major symphonic work, *Enigma Variations*, written in 1898, that established him firmly as a serious new voice in British music.

After composing his 'Sea Pictures' in 1899 came one of Elgar's most impressive choral works, *The Dream of Gerontius*, based on the poem by Catholic Cardinal John Newman. The premiere, composed for the Birmingham Music Festival of 1900, was a bit of a debacle, the choir being under-rehearsed and the soloists not up to much. And things didn't get any better – the piece's overtly

Roman Catholic tone caused disquiet among Anglican clerics, so much so that it was banned by various Anglican churches for some years. However, it was received very well at its premiere in Germany at the end of 1901.

The early 1900s were his most creative years, his cantatas *The Apostles* and *The Kingdom*, composed from 1901 to 1906, and the first performance of his impressive First Symphony No. 1 in A-flat Major was performed in Manchester in 1908. To add to his triumphs, he was knighted in 1904 by Edward VII. The Violin Concerto in B Minor followed in 1910, and a year later he composed his second symphony, No. 2 in E-flat Major.

The war years depressed Elgar to the point where he was unable to compose more than a few patriotic pieces; his great masterpiece, the Cello Concerto in E Minor, coming in 1919, along with three other chamber works.

With the death of his wife, much of the spirit went out of Elgar's life, and he lived in semi-retirement. He did conduct most of his works for recordings, and there was somewhat of a resurgence of composition, though two major works were incomplete at the time of his death – an opera, *The Spanish Lady*, and a third symphony.

Recommended listening

Elgar wrote some lovely songs for unaccompanied soprano, alto, tenor and bass (SATB). Two of them, 'The Fountain' and 'The Shower', were written to words by the metaphysical poet Henry Vaughan. 'The Shower' is a reflective song with deep harmonies and sustained notes, interspersed with short semiquaver phrases representing drops of rain, the last chords indicating that the shower is over. 'The Fountain' begins with a happy burst of sound, almost as if a fountain has just been switched on. There's a more reflective central theme, which returns to a slower version of the first melody again.

GRACE NOTE

Elgar was a keen Wolverhampton Wanderers fan.

MAHLER, GUSTAV (1860-1911)

Gustav Mahler was known more for his conducting than his compositions during his lifetime, being regarded as one of the world's best, and it's only through the attentions of prominent musicians, such as Leonard Bernstein and Otto Klemperer, that his works have received the attention they deserve.

Jewish Mahler was born in Bohemia; his parents' marriage was unhappy but they did stop quarrelling long enough for his father to be aware of his musical talent. Consequently, the rather brooding young man entered the Vienna Conservatory when he was 15, the composer Hugo Wolf being a fellow pupil. Though he was a good pianist, he spent the next few years supporting himself as a conductor in various provincial theatres. But his conducting talent eventually led to appointments in Prague; Leipzig, where he composed his first symphony; the Royal Opera in Budapest; and Hamburg, where he conducted Wagner's *Tristan and Isolde*. His stay in Hamburg was not without its tensions, his demanding rehearsal schedules were resented by the orchestra and vocalists alike. He moved to Vienna in 1897 to conduct at the Vienna Court Opera, and remained there for ten years. He composed when he could, usually in the summer at his lakeside retreat.

In 1907, his poor working relationship with artistes, his demanding standards and the pressure on him by anti-Semitic factions in Vienna led to his resignation.

Although Mahler is best remembered for his nine great symphonies, his first notable works were actually song cycles, written around 1884: *Lieder eines fahrenden Gesellen* (*Songs of a Wayfarer*) and, based on a collection of German poetry, *Des Knaben Wunderhorn* (*The Youth's Magic Horn*).

Dying young, he was only lauded for his conducting; his symphonies were regarded as little more than added extras.

Recommended listening

His symphony No. 1 in D Major, the third movement of which features a rather sombre version of the nursery rhyme Frère Jacques.

DEBUSSY, CLAUDE (1862-1918)

Debussy once said that music is made up of colours and rhythms, and that it shouldn't be confined to rigid musical forms. Certainly he was a one-off amongst his late Romantic contemporaries, his work with new harmonies and beautifully dissonant chords often being described as Impressionist (after the painters' misty style), a term he loathed – maybe because that was a label, and if nothing else Debussy was never to be labelled.

He didn't start piano lessons until he was seven but he made such staggering progress that by the age of ten he was enrolled at the Paris Conservatory. In 1884, he won the institution's Prix de Rome (a scholarship for arts students), but his stay in Rome was not happy as everyone was obsessed with opera, and their formal musical constructions were just not Debussy's thing.

He was, however, moved by the sensuality and the mastery of Wagner's operas when he visited Bayreuth in 1888, and the Javanese gamelan music Debussy heard at the 1889 Paris World Exposition left a great impression. If you listen to his 'Pagodes' piano piece, you can really hear the gamelan influence.

He often turned to poetry for inspiration, too; his *Suite Bergamasque*, of which the lovely 'Clair de Lune' is a movement, was inspired by a poem written by Paul Verlaine, who was part of the French Symbolist arts movement.

But it was Stéphane Marllarmé's poem that inspired the composition which challenged the musical rulebook and set critics' tongues wagging. His 1894 instrumental song, 'Prélude à l'après-Midi d'un Faune' ('Prelude to the Afternoon of a Faun'), with its unusual musical structure and texture, was described by one critic as 'a curious fantasy, full of unprecise [sic] harmonics and fleeting phrases'.

Debussy composed very slowly and meticulously, and over the next few years his output was slow, producing his opera *Pelléas and Mélisande*, his three orchestral nocturnes – 'Nuages' ('Clouds'), 'Fêtes' ('Festivals') and 'Sirènes' ('Sirens') inspired by the paintings of Whistler – and other piano works. Although 'Faun' had gained some attention, it wasn't until his nocturnes were published that the public took notice of the composer, although he was still making hardly any money from his work.

His three symphonic sketches, collectively titled *La Mer* (*The Sea*) – part-symphony, part-tone poem – composed in 1905, didn't go down too well either, but that could have been in part because he'd not long ago caused a scandal in leaving his wife, who rather publicly tried to commit suicide in Paris' Place de la Concorde, for another woman. Debussy and his pregnant mistress fled to Eastbourne where *La Mer* was completed. With his complicated love life, no wonder it took an age to get the notes down.

Recommended listening

The second movement of his 'Estampes' ('Prints') piano solo and 'Pagodes', with its reflective oriental influences.

RACHMANINOFF, SERGEI (1873-1943)

'A composer's music should express
the country of his birth.'

... and, as one of the last great Russian Romantic composers, Rachmaninoff made sure his music did just that. Yet just around the corner from the sweeping melodies, so reminiscent of his idol, Tchaikovsky, and the lush, richly textured harmonies of his brooding Prelude in C-sharp Minor, waited the modern works of composers such as Stravinsky and Shostakovich – a world of difference in just a few short years. Rachmaninoff, on the other hand, stayed loyal to his Romantic nature.

He was one of if not *the* greatest pianist of the twentieth century, whose talents equalled those of Liszt, and whose piano works are fiendishly difficult to play. He had huge hands, with an enormous span, so he was able to play very difficult chord constructions. But he was also very deft, as an old recording of his playing Nikolai Rimsky-Korsakov's 'Flight of the Bumblebee' testifies.

Although he was born into a wealthy family, his father frittered it all away and Rachmaninoff entered Saint Petersburg Conservatory on a scholarship. His parents separated, his sister died, so not surprisingly he failed his exams. Entering the Moscow Conservatory, the regime was strict but it obviously did the trick as he passed his final piano exam in 1891 with honours.

The dramatic forte octaves which open his Piano Concerto No. 1 (written in 1891) are in marked contrast to the subdued but increasingly intense chord openers of his Piano Concerto No. 2 (1900). It's a wonder, though, that the latter was ever written; the premiere of his first symphony had been a disaster and was savaged by the critics. For the next three years, Rachmaninoff had writer's block but after a course of therapy he began to compose again, this second piano concerto the result – a work that helped to establish him as a composer and which is still much loved today.

A stint as conductor of the Bolshoi Theatre in the early 1890s and three winters in Dresden composing was followed by a tour of America as a pianist in 1909. He returned to the Soviet Union the following year.

Political turbulence in Russia in 1918 forced Rachmaninoff and his family to leave; they eventually settled in America which became his home until his death in 1943.

Recommended listening

Rachmaninoff's *Rhapsody on a Theme of Paganini*. The piece, based on a set of 24 variations on the twenty-fourth and last of Paganini's Caprices for solo violin, struck a chord with many composers, including Liszt and Brahms. Rachmaninoff's version was written in the 1930s when romanticism was rapidly becoming passé. Perhaps this was a stab at using a classical theme in a new way...

STRAUSS, RICHARD (1864–1949)

*'I may not be a first-rate composer,
but I am a first-class second-rate composer.'*

Not the waltz chap, Johann II, who was around a bit earlier, from 1825 to 1899, and whose lightweight waltzes would be no match for Richard's heavier, large scale pieces. Strauss wrote tone poems, operas and loved Wagner's music as much as his father – a horn player and a bit of a conservative – hated it, and he was a conductor to boot. His first musical breakthrough came with the symphonic tone poem 'Don Juan', and fired up by this, he wrote a series of others. Later on, he turned his attention to opera, raising eyebrows with *Salome* in 1905 (with all that biblical naughtiness) and *Elektra* (with death and revenge) in 1909.

He was always a bit hidebound by Wagner, but that changed with his 1911 comic opera, *Der Rosenkavalier*, which received rave reviews.

The war years were difficult, largely spent trying to protect his Jewish relatives, but he continued to compose well into his eighties. His Metamorphosen, Study for 23 Strings, completed in 1945, is a dramatic, sprawling work, lamenting the destruction of Germany. His *Last Four Songs* collection, 'Frühling' ('Spring'), 'September', 'Beim Schlafengehen' ('When Falling Asleep') and 'Im Abendrot' ('At Sunset'), composed in 1948, are magnificent, especially 'Im Abendrot'.

Recommended listening

Strauss never lived to hear his *Last Four Songs* performed but if he had, he would have been proud to have known that such stars as Renèe Fleming, Jessye Norman and the incomparable Elisabeth Schwarzkopf would one day sing them.

RAVEL, MAURICE (1875-1937)

Like Debussy, Ravel was French, he lived at around the same time and was considered an Impressionist composer, but the two men could hardly be more different musically. Whereas Debussy's music flows wild and free, Ravel's composition is more precisely written. But drawn to his mother's Basque and Spanish heritage, his work is full of the regions' rhythms and melodies. This can be clearly discerned in his *Rhapsodie Espagnole* (1907) or his *Boléro* (1928).

Although he had piano lessons, Ravel seemed more interested in composing but, nevertheless, went to the Paris Conservatory around 1889 to study piano. However, he was expelled for failing to meet standards in 1895 and it was around this time that he composed the charming little piano piece 'Menuet Antique'. He did eventually return to the conservatoire for a while a bit later on, in order to study composition with Fauré.

Around 1905, things got rather nasty at the conservatoire – Ravel had tried several times to win the prestigious Prix de Rome and failed yet again to reach the finals. Accusations of preferential treatment of one of the judges' students abounded, factions arose, and the conservatoire director resigned. The scandal was named the 'Ravel Affair' in the press.

But, as with many composers, the incident seemed to have fired his imagination, as the next years proved fruitful for Ravel: two piano works, the fabulously flowing 'Sonatine', and the suite, *Miroirs,* which has depth and brilliant key-changing dissonances and rhythmic patterns. In 1909, Diaghilev commissioned Ravel to score the ballet *Daphnis et Chloé,* followed by *Ma Mère l'Oye* (*Mother Goose*).

Turned down for active service in World War One, he became an ambulance driver on the Western front but, in 1916, his health deteriorated upon the death of his mother and, in 1921, he retired to the country where he continued to compose. Seven years later, in 1928, he began a tour of America, being particularly impressed with the jazz scene of New Orleans. You can really hear the jazz influences in his Piano Concerto in G Major which he composed between 1929 and 1930. Interestingly, his other piano concerto, written at the same time, was a Piano Concerto for the Left Hand, commissioned by a pianist who had lost his right arm during the war.

In 1928, Ravel wrote his famous *Boléro*, and visions of Torvill and Dean notwithstanding, he had a famous falling-out with conductor Arturo Toscanini over his version of it. 'Too fast,' said Ravel. 'It's the only way to save the work,' said Toscanini.

Recommended listening

'Pavane pour une Infante Défunte' ('Pavane for a Dead Princess'), written in 1899, when Ravel was studying with Fauré. Originally for piano, Ravel published an orchestral version too. Again, this has Spanish influences.

VAUGHAN WILLIAMS, RALPH (1872-1958)

Vaughan Williams' work falls very much into the 'traditional' bracket; it has a powerful, noble and distinctly 'English' style, being as he was a prodigious collector of English folk tunes. Indeed, his profound interest in them shaped his compositions; he made numerous arrangements of many of them, some as hymn tunes (reflecting his editorship of *The English Hymnal* from 1906).

Born in the Gloucestershire village of Down Ampney (after which he would later title his tune to the hymn 'Come Down, O Love Divine'), he showed early musical talent at the piano and went off to the Royal College of Music (RCM) in 1890, becoming a pupil of the composer Hubert Parry.

He carried on his composition studies at Trinity College, Cambridge, before returning to the RCM. There he made great friends with Gustav Holst, whom Vaughan Williams spoke of as a 'great influence' on his music.

He was 30 before his first song, 'Linden Lea', was published, but in 1904 his discovery of an English folk song 'Bushes and Briars' made a permanent impact on his work and eventually led to a resurgence of interest in traditional tunes.

The years before World War One saw some of his major works including the song cycle *On Wenlock Edge*; *Fantasia on a Theme by Thomas Tallis*, which reflected his love of Renaissance music; his choral *A Sea Symphony*, based on poems by Walt Whitman; and *A London Symphony*, which was composed in 1914.

During the war Vaughan Williams joined the Army Medical Corps as a stretcher-bearer, his experiences leading to the composition of his haunting Third Symphony; there's a trumpet solo in the second movement (about 14 minutes in) based on his hearing a bugler practising.

After World War One, Vaughan Williams went back to the RCM to teach; he was president of the Bach Choir from the mid 1940s and, in later life, president of the English Folk Dance and Song Society. Key works from the post-war period include further symphonies – he wrote nine in all – such as Mass in G Minor, 'The Lark Ascending' (regularly at the top of the classical hit parade) and the sublime 'Serenade to Music'. There are loads more, including his opera *The Pilgrim's Progress* and the ever-popular piece 'Fantasia on "Greensleeves"'.

Recommended listening

'Serenade to Music' is a work for 16 vocal soloists and an orchestra based on lines from *The Merchant of Venice*, and dedicated to Henry Wood (he of the Proms).

The song 'Silent Noon' is based on a Gabriel Rossetti sonnet. 'Your hands lie open in the long fresh grass, / The finger-points look through like rosy blooms: / Your eyes smile peace.' The music flows with syncopated chords leading to a piu mosso (quicker) section, its arpeggio quavers sweeping the music along and perfectly complementing Rossetti's words.

GRACE NOTE

Vaughan Williams' mother was Margaret Wedgwood, the great-granddaughter of the potter Josiah.

MUSIC, MUSIC, MUSIC: CHORUSES AND CONCERTOS

From Handel's triumphant *Zadok the Priest* to the hellfire of Verdi's Requiem, from the haunting second movement of Mozart's clarinet concerto to the majesty of Beethoven's 'Emperor' piano concerto, here are just some of the finest choral and instrumental works to add to your classical music collection.

CHORAL WORKS

THE CREATION, HAYDN

Although known principally for his symphonies and his string quartets, Haydn was no slouch at oratorio, even though he wrote only two – *The Creation* (1798), acclaimed by many to be his finest masterpiece, and *The Seasons* (1801). He wrote them after one of his trips to London, and on hearing Handel's oratorios, he wanted to write something on the scale of *Israel in Egypt*.

The Creation's libretto – a poem entitled 'The Creation of the World' (author unknown) – was based on Milton's *Paradise Lost*, The Book of Genesis and Psalms. The first two parts of the oratorio describe the six days of the Creation and part three takes place in the Garden of Eden, so there's a lot to listen to.

Haydn had a talent for orchestral 'colour' – the long introduction, The Representation of Chaos, has crashing chords and flute-like phrases, and the strings' pulse brings a real sense of the struggle for the light. After the chorus quietly sings 'Let there be light', the sound simply blazes out. There's also an impressive soprano aria 'On mighty wings' that celebrates the creation of birds.

ZADOK THE PRIEST, HANDEL

If there's one composer who knew how to keep the listener in suspense, it was Handel with *Zadok the Priest*; the arpeggio strings building slowly until the first triumphal entry of the choir, a full one and a half minutes in. This piece was one of four anthems composed for King George's coronation in 1727 – perhaps it was a Royal nod of assent from the king himself, as Handel received British citizenship the same year.

ST MATTHEW PASSION, BACH

Bach wrote this in 1727 for soloists, a double choir and two orchestras, and it's one of his grandest and most popular works. Although he revised it a couple of times in subsequent years, it was first performed in Leipzig on the Good Friday of that year. Its powerful blend of narration, huge choruses and intimate arias gives the story of Saint Matthew's account of Jesus' betrayal and crucifixion a startling emotional intensity, which is almost operatic in places. The story is told by the Evangelist, Jesus,

Pontius Pilate and other soloists. Bach adds a 'halo' of expressive string accompaniment to distinguish Jesus from the other characters and he uses musical devices such as this throughout to reinforce the words. Some say it's baroque at its finest.

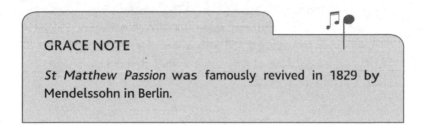

GRACE NOTE

St Matthew Passion was famously revived in 1829 by Mendelssohn in Berlin.

MESSIAH, HANDEL

Beloved of every choral society up and down the country at Christmas, this oratorio is possibly one of the greatest of great choral works. Yet, highlights during the festive season notwithstanding, this deserves to be heard in its entirety, as there's a lot more to it than the 'Hallelujah' chorus and 'For unto us a child is born'.

There's a beautiful balance between choruses and arias, especially as there are fewer recitatives than in many oratorios of the period. Handel shows clever use of notation – in the aria 'Every valley shall be exalted', Handel scores the quavers as a rapid four-figure pattern for the words 'the crooked straight', and there is a series of longer, smoother notes to denote 'the rough places plain'. Every chorus is a gem but 'Glory to God', 'All we, like sheep, have gone astray' and the contrasting 'Since by man came death' are spectacular. 'I know that my Redeemer liveth' is probably one of the best known soprano arias, and, the soprano and alto duet 'He shall feed his flock like a shepherd' is graceful and balanced.

GRACE NOTE

Handel wrote *Messiah* in 1741 and it was premiered in Dublin a year later. However, we might have missed out on this glorious oratorio, as in 1703, Handel was nearly killed in a duel with composer Johann Mattheson. They were close friends but had a sudden quarrel; Handel was only saved because Mattheson's sword glanced off a large button on Handel's coat.

REQUIEM MASS IN D MINOR, MOZART

There was once an air of mystery surrounding the story of the requiem's unknown commissioner in the spring of 1792, and certainly the ailing Mozart thought this was to be the requiem that would commemorate his own death. It is now known that the work was commissioned by Franz von Walsegg who, by all accounts, had a habit of commissioning works which he tried to pass off as his own. As we know, Mozart died before completing the work, having only reached the Lacrimosa before shuffling off the mortal coil.

The bass lead into the magnificent Kyrie is a startling introduction, which leads to intricate ducking and diving of the long choral phrases. The drama of the Dies Irae, the contrasts of mood in Confutatis and the rather sad, moving notes of the Lacrimosa were the last that Mozart ever wrote. Have the tissues handy.

MESSA DA REQUIEM (REQUIEM MASS), VERDI

For a man so steeped in opera – although after the composition of *Aida* in 1871 he didn't write any for 16 years – it is interesting that one of Verdi's most important pieces was a sacred work. It was in 1874 when he brought all of his operatic know-how to this requiem, which became a composition of dramatic proportions.

If you're looking for a work of salvation and peace then try Fauré's Requiem. Verdi is the fire and brimstone man, and parts of his requiem are hair-raising; the Dies Irae, for example, encompasses the full orchestra, preceded by four striking string chords. There are moments of quiet reflection in the Lacrimosa, too. It is a work of immense proportions and is utterly moving.

MISSA SOLEMNIS (SOLEMN MASS) IN D MAJOR, BEETHOVEN

Beethoven began writing this Mass in April 1819 for the consecration of his pupil Archduke Rudolph as Archbishop of Olmütz, but it wasn't completed until 1824. Beethoven is probably regarded as a composer full of thunder and drama (his Fifth Symphony, for example) and we can certainly hear his power in the huge fugues in the Gloria and the Credo. But then there is such a contrast in the lyrical Benedictus, which begins with a violin solo that weaves in and out of the following quartet and the chorus, and through to the end of the section. Impressive, too, is the 'Dona nobis pacem' ('Grant us peace') which has an almost folk-tune sounding melody. Rather than being all power and volume, this is a work which is memorable on many levels – as Beethoven was.

DIDO AND AENEAS, PURCELL

This is a gem of an opera, composed *c*.1688. Just like the 'Hallelujah' chorus from *Messiah*, all that is ever played from this composition is the aria, Dido's Lament, 'When I am laid in earth', which is a great pity. It's a story of tragic lovers and a sorceress who spoils their happiness. Aeneas, torn between love and duty, sails off into the sunset while Dido awaits death. Surprisingly, it is very jaunty in parts, for example the sorceress and the witches have a great time with their recitatives and choruses at the beginning of act two, and in the sailors' chorus which opens act three – 'take a boozy short leave of your nymphs on the shore…'. But there is that ground bass of the lament, which has been called the most exquisite ever composed. It is a tale of sailors, witches, shepherds and shepherdesses, heroes and villains, and all penned more than 300 years ago. Remarkable.

CONCERTOS

CLARINET CONCERTO IN A MAJOR, K 622, MOZART

Musical liquid gold – especially the second movement which is a moving legato melody of infinite beauty underscored by a smooth and understated strings accompaniment. The third rondo movement is a cheerful romp, the clarinet melody having fast semiquaver (short note) passages which allows the clarinettist to show off their dexterity. This is a lovely concerto, which was written in 1791, shortly before Mozart's death in the same year, and published posthumously.

PIANO CONCERTO NO. 1 IN B-FLAT MINOR, TCHAIKOVSKY

If ever there was an introduction to the power and drama of Tchaikovsky's writing, this is it. After the French horn's imperious four-note introduction, the pianist takes charge with those familiar, stirringly dramatic chords stepping from one end of the piano to the other. This concerto includes peaceful, reflective moments to catch your breath, legato strings and phrases of lyrical beauty in the second movement, and a fiery con fuoco in the third.

PIANO CONCERTO NO. 5 IN E-FLAT MAJOR ('EMPEROR'), BEETHOVEN

The first movement is a majestic tour de force – if you ever wondered why pianists practise scales and arpeggios, the first bars of the pianist's solo here are the reason. Following massive themes and a massive first movement, the second is so delicate and sad, the contrast is almost unbearable, though compelling. The third movement is a rondo and another exuberant powerhouse of an exchange between piano and orchestra. It is stunning in its musical depth and breadth.

LE QUATTRO STAGIONI (THE FOUR SEASONS), VIVALDI

These four violin concertos, written at the end of 1725, are part of a group of 12 concertos and are certainly the most well known. The four pieces are accompanied by brief sonnets, describing the seasons. Listen out for the pizzicato strings of winter – the sting of icy sleet, perhaps? And long violin notes give a sense of the laid-back languor of summer.

CONCERTO FOR MANDOLIN AND STRINGS IN C MAJOR, VIVALDI

Probably unusual to put this in the list but it is a joyful piece, and the mandolin has a pleasing, unusual sound. The whole concerto is only about nine minutes long and is scored for mandolin, strings and continuo. The first movement, which is only about three minutes long, starts off at a romp. The contrasting slow second movement ends with a stately, pizzicato into the third. Vivaldi's Concerto for Two Mandolins in G is also notable – the third movement is three in a bar and has an excellent sense of movement.

CONCERTO FOR TWO VIOLINS IN D MINOR, BACH

The majestically fluid opening movement is pure Bach and the relationship between the two violins and the orchestra is a masterclass. The second largo movement is poetry, one violin beginning the theme, the second soaring in over the first, and the melody lines weaving between the two. The finale is an allegro which propels the piece on to the end. The concerto has it all – fugues, counterpoint and a beautiful musical balance. Not a lot more you could ask for.

CELLO CONCERTO IN E MINOR, OP. 85, ELGAR

This concerto was written by Edward Elgar in 1919, in his summerhouse 'Brinkwells', near Fittleworth in Sussex. It is ironic that this piece, which is now loved by so many for its moving elegance, seemed almost ill-fated at first. Elgar retired to Fittleworth, unhappy in the knowledge that the post-World

War One world seemed to have moved on from his music; and the concerto had a disastrous premiere. But, historical difficulties forgotten, you will be transfixed from the minute the solo cello bow first sweeps across the strings.

PIANO CONCERTO NO. 2, OP. 16, RACHMANINOFF

Oh, the romance, the lush chords, the sweeping violins… There's a section of delicate piano 'raindrops' in the right hand about five minutes into the first movement which will have you fall in love with the composer for that alone.

THE CLASSICAL CONSUMER

ARE YOU SITTING COMFORTABLY?

Before considering the dos and don'ts of going to a concert, it may be worth mentioning that many years ago audiences weren't always on their best behaviour – far from it. Although they wouldn't have thought of it as bad manners at the time…

In the baroque era, music was still the preserve of royal households and a public concert was unheard of even at the beginning of the eighteenth century. Gradually, however, music became the fashionable pursuit of the upper classes and by the time the classical orchestra evolved, composers began to make a living independent of the church or the court, and so concerts began to be held in public. For example, Vauxhall Gardens in eighteenth-century London became *the* place to be seen for amusement and music.

Today, the mark of a music-savvy audience is the lack of clapping between movements – eager, perhaps, to show those less well-informed that they are aware the piece hasn't yet finished. But this is a twentieth-century convention. The audiences in the days of Mozart and Haydn would be puzzled by this as, not only did they clap between movements, a loud appreciation of the music was encouraged by composers who played to noisy audiences having dinner, drinking, chatting or generally kicking up a rumpus.

In a letter to his father in 1778, Mozart waxed lyrical about the wild applause he received during one of his symphonies: 'I was so delighted, I went right after the Sinfonie to the Palais Royale – bought myself an ice cream, prayed a rosary as I had pledged – and went home.'

It was Richard Wagner who first mooted the idea of attentive listening and clamped down on applause between movements, while Mahler, for his part, wasn't very happy with certain sections of an audience that were paid to applaud a favourite singer. As recording technology became more sophisticated and concerts began to be recorded live, applause began to be seen as a distraction and a faux pas.

A SHORT (AND PAINLESS) GUIDE TO CONCERT ETIQUETTE

'Great music is sound, painted on
a canvas of silence.'
LEOPOLD STOKOWSKI

Going to a classical music concert is always a great experience – the buzz of the audience, the cacophony of sound as the orchestra tunes up and the arrival of the principal players. To help you get the most from your evening, here are a few important pointers:

ARRIVE ON TIME

Try not to be late – sometimes it's unavoidable but you may well be refused entry if you are. Nobody wants to listen to the squeak of seats going up and down or whispered 'Excuse me's' and 'Sorry's' once the concert has begun. You'll probably have to wait until the end of the first piece, or even until the interval, to take your seats. However, kind ushers might allow you to sit on a vacant seat at the back of the stalls when there is a suitable pause in the music.

DON'T PHONE HOME

Musicians have spent a lot of time, expertise and effort to bring you beautiful music and won't want to hear a mobile phone blasting out the Test Match Special or *Close Encounters of the Third Kind* theme. Remember to put your phone on silent or, better still, switch it off, or you may find yourself having a close encounter with a member of front-of-house staff showing you the exit.

HALF-TIME DRINKS

Don't unwrap sweets, slurp drinks or ferret around for your favourite chocolate from the box. It's distracting in the silent bits and discourteous to those around you. You can indulge in the Belgian truffles at the interval.

A QUIET WORD

Coughing, sneezing, chatting, programme-wafting, music score-following (how is it nobody can turn a page quietly?), head-nodding, foot-tapping. All these can be off-putting for performers who need to focus; and the one thing concertgoers want to do is to listen to the music undisturbed, so it's a no-brainer to try to keep the fidgeting down to a minimum. Handkerchiefs at the ready.

It's also a thorny question as to whether young children should be taken to an 'adult' concert. The Korean violinist Kyung-Wha Chung made headlines in December 2014 when she suggested to the parents of a restless, coughing child that she 'should be brought back when she was older'. It may be she had a point in that it was unfair to ask a child to sit still and quietly for so long.

Tilson Thomas, music director of the San Francisco Symphony, most famously stopped Mahler's Ninth Symphony mid-performance to lob two handfuls of cough drops at a chronically coughing audience. It's also said that John Barbirolli halted a concert because the clacking of a woman's knitting needles in the audience was affecting his concentration.

I'll leave the final comments on this subject to Oliver Pritchett of *The Telegraph*:

> '*It is that sense of danger you experience as you look along your row of seats and see someone's chest gradually swelling and his eyes beginning to bulge and his mouth twisting and you know there is a cough in there and it is going to have to come out during the piano solo. Just beyond him, you see the lady who has been holding back a sneeze for the past 32 bars; her index finger is pressed under her nose and eyes are watering. The suspense is… exquisite.*'

DRESSING FOR THE OCCASION

There are no hard-and-fast rules about what to wear to a concert – it depends on where you're going. The Royal Opera House? La Scala? Vienna's New Year concert? Then an elegant frock, or a DJ or lounge suit, is the only way to go. It's common sense really, but if you'd spent a good part of the year mustering your choir into shape for its annual Christmas concert, would you want your audience turning up in ripped jeans or a tracksuit? And one for the ladies – don't pile your hair up in a sky-high style (really, some do) or you may have the person in the seat behind you parting your backcombed coiffure down the middle for a better view.

TO CLAP OR NOT TO CLAP, THAT IS THE QUESTION

It seems the thing newbie concertgoers worry about most is when to clap. Well, don't. Worry that is. Imagine you're at a posh dinner and there's a frightening array of knives and forks in serried ranks next to your place mat. Which do you use? Don't panic, just wait and see which ones everyone else picks up. Ditto a classical concert – take your lead from your fellow concertgoers, notice what they're doing. The general rule of thumb is if they clap, you can, too.

The audience will often applaud when the orchestra leader, then the conductor and the soloists, walk onstage. Symphonies, concertos and the like are divided into movements and it's accepted as the norm that you don't clap between movements, as the music – movements and all – is regarded as a 'whole'.

There is a good deal of comment nowadays about where and when to applaud, but whatever the feeling on the matter, one thing is for sure, nothing can compare at the end of a musical performance to those breathless moments of silent reflective delight before the audience commences the applause and the 'Bravos!'.

BUT... AND IT'S A BIG BUT

Having said all this, if you have ever been to the ballet or to an opera, you will know that not only will an audience applaud (and cheer) a particularly impressive operatic solo mid-scene, or a ballet solo or a *pas de deux*, the artist will acknowledge the audience and take a bow. One would think it would ruin the artist's concentration, but it is established form to do this.

SO, WHEN IN DOUBT...

Only one rule applies – wait and see what everyone else does.

GRACE NOTE

Carl Maria von Weber's piano composition 'Invitation to the Dance' often catches audiences out because the piece, which tells the story of a couple at a ball, has a false ending. Usually, though, any conductor worth his salt will take it on the chin, and you might just get away with a humorous finger wagging!

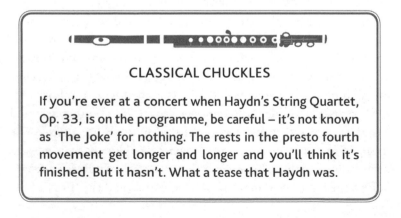

CLASSICAL CHUCKLES

If you're ever at a concert when Haydn's String Quartet, Op. 33, is on the programme, be careful – it's not known as 'The Joke' for nothing. The rests in the presto fourth movement get longer and longer and you'll think it's finished. But it hasn't. What a tease that Haydn was.

BLURRING THE BOUNDARIES

IT'S CLASSICAL, IT'S POP, IT'S JAZZ

Although the classical purists would probably disagree, the twentieth century and beyond has seen the welcome and, for the most part, extremely clever melding of classical and modern music. For example, who would have thought that the duet 'Barcelona', written for the Barcelona Olympics in 1992 and sung by the unlikely combination of international soprano Montserrat Caballé and Queen's Freddie Mercury, would have struck such a chord worldwide?

Actress and light entertainer Joyce Grenfell recorded a series of different 'pretend' classical encores (as a comedy sketch) for those artists '… with hope in their hearts and sometimes they actually get to use them but I'm not a real singer and I can't afford to take any chances, so I've got five…' and she sings encores for five different singers, from the nervous school concert chorister to the 'foreign visitor to our shores'.

Alan Sherman's 'Hello Mudder, Hello Fadda' was a novelty song he recorded in 1963 to the tune of Italian composer Amilcare Ponchielli's *Dance of the Hours*.

Sometimes, then, it's difficult – and tantalising – to work out where classical music ends and popular music begins.

AND ALL THAT JAZZ…

Jazz and classical music – can they work together? They certainly did when eminent classical violinist Yehudi Menuhin played violin with jazz violinist Stéphane Grappelli – look out for a YouTube clip of them playing 'Jealousy' together. In the clip, Menuhin says that he learned every note, and yet it sounds spontaneous and full of joy. That duet led to them making several albums together.

Another jazz classicist is French pianist Jacques Loussier, who formed the Jacques Loussier Trio, famed worldwide for jazzing up the works of Bach with a series of *Play Bach* albums. The lineup of the trio has changed over the years (Jacques is now the only original left) but the quality of the trio's playing has not. The relaxing Siciliano in G Minor or the Toccata and Fugue in D Minor will give you an idea of Loussier's unique and sophisticated approach to Bach.

The jazz clarinettist Benny Goodman commissioned Aaron Copland, who composed *Appalachian Spring*, to write him a clarinet concerto, which premiered in 1950.

Classical violinist Itzhak Perlman collaborated with jazz pianist Oscar Peterson to make the 1994 album *Side by Side*. Tracks include the 1939 bluesy song 'Stormy Weather', Irving Berlin's 'Blue Skies' and 'I Loves You, Porgy', originally a duet from George Gershwin's opera *Porgy and Bess*.

The Swingle Singers, from Paris, were formed by Ward Swingle (1927–2015) in 1962 and were originally famous for their versions of 'swinging' Bach. Although these days the group sings compositions other than Bach's, the renamed Swingles is still going strong.

'Classical pop' ensembles are very much the thing, with groups such as Il Divo, the OperaBabes and Amici Forever enjoying great success. The King's Singers could be considered as the group that started this all off. Formed in 1968, the six-member group sings a delightful mix of different music, from classical, sacred and madrigals, to folk, ballad and pop. That they take on such a hugely diverse repertoire in no way dilutes any particular style – they tackle everything with great *joie de vivre*!

CLASSICAL CROSSOVER

There's always been a bit of a debate as to whether classical singers can 'cross over' to sing pop, and vice versa. A tricky one; as it's not *just* about the classical voice having to be powerful enough to be heard at the back of the hall (and over an orchestra) while the pop artist has a mic to amplify the sound – the technique to sing both styles is completely different.

A classical singer has to sing every note true (rather than taking a step up to a note, which is a familiar pop technique). A classical singer also sings through to the end of each beat, using their diaphragm to support the sound, which is essential when they're singing a long, sustained note. A pop singer, on the other hand, will often sing through the beat and on the breath, and would probably find it quite difficult to sing very long or sustained notes and phrases. Little wonder then that those who have crossed over from one genre to the other have found it a challenge.

Musical theatre star Barbra Streisand has recorded the lovely 'Après un Rêve' ('After a Dream') by Fauré, Schubert's 'Who is Sylvia', and one of Joseph Canteloube's *Songs of the Auvergne*, all being very well received.

One of the most interesting crossovers from classical to modern was the (perhaps rather unlikely) collaboration between the operatic mezzo-soprano Anne Sofie von Otter and her ardent fan Elvis Costello: the album *For the Stars*, the result. Despite being produced by Costello and with input from former ABBA member Benny Andersson, von Otter insisted it was not a pop album but a mix of chamber, classical, folk and pop. It's a moving, interesting result: Anne-Sofie obviously at home singing within herself into a mic. The tracks 'Like an Angel Passing Through My Room' and 'Green Song' show off her voice very well.

WHERE HAVE I HEARD THAT TUNE?

Composers of pop songs have long since used phrases or repeating patterns from classical music to enhance their compositions. Is it their way of paying homage to the genius of composers long dead? Or is it that modern writers find classical themes too good to resist?

The rock band Procol Harum's 'A Whiter Shade of Pale', which uses Bach's melody line from his 'Air on the G String', was released in May 1967 and reached number one the following month, staying there for six weeks – and it's still on radio playlists now.

Interestingly, you can go a good deal further back than the 1960s to find recycled classical themes in popular music. The vaudeville song 'I'm Always Chasing Rainbows' was written in 1917 by Harry Carroll and has been sung by many artists over the years, including Judy Garland in the film *Ziegfeld Girl*. But maybe the credit should go to Chopin, as the melody is based on his 'Fantaisie-Impromptu' – you'll find the tune about one minute in.

Several pop stars of the 1950s and 1960s picked up on melodies from classical music, including Perry Como's 'Catch a Falling Star' (Brahms' 'Academic Festival Overture', albeit a loose variation, about five minutes in) and Elvis Presley's 'It's Now or Never' melody line comes from 'O Sole Mio', a song composed by Eduardo di Capua in 1898 (and it's also the theme tune of 'Just One Cornetto').

More recently, the 2013 song 'Love is a Bourgeois Construct', from pop duo the Pet Shop Boys, has an intriguing history in its repeating riff, which comes from English composer Michael Nyman's music for the 1982 film *The Draughtsman's Contract*. The film is set around 1694, during the reign of William and Mary, and Nyman's music is very much a Purcell–Nyman mix; he studied and borrowed Purcell's musical forms but makes the music his own. It's a really good soundtrack and worth a listen.

RADIO, TELEVISION AND THE BIG SCREEN

WHERE'S THE REMOTE?

It's never been easier to listen to classical music because there's a whole world of music at your fingertips – you don't even have to leave your armchair. Press the digital radio button, hook up to Radio 3 or Classic FM, iTunes, Spotify or YouTube on your phone, computer or tablet and listen to great music when you like, as you like.

THIS IS THE BBC THIRD PROGRAMME

'The Third Programme will... devote to the great works the time they require. Its whole content will be directed to an audience that is not of one class but that is perceptive and intelligent.'

So said William Haley, the BBC director-general, in September 1946 at the launch of the BBC's Third Programme.

There was the need for a radio station that could present a 'great classical repertoire in music, literature and other arts', and the Third Programme filled this gap; it wasn't something that could be done on the BBC Home Service (begun in 1939) or the Light Programme (launched in 1945) – classical music and the arts needed a dedicated radio station.

Something like this had been mooted as long ago as the 1920s, when radio broadcasting had first begun, but it had not been greeted with much enthusiasm by the BBC's first director-general, John Reith, who preferred a rather more 'mixed up' output. However, there were some very popular classical music talks and concerts broadcast between 1926 and 1939, including Henry Walford Davies' series *Music and the Ordinary Listener*. But Reith was not for turning.

After his departure in 1938, BBC radio muddled along until a growing appetite for the arts necessitated another look at the possibility of a third dedicated radio station.

So the Third Programme was launched and was broadcast for 6 hours each evening – an eclectic mix of music and words, live concerts, contemporary music, jazz and drama productions. On the Light Programme, during the day, were programmes such as *Bandstand, Music While You Work, Mrs Dale's Diary, Dick Barton – Special Agent, Wilfred Pickles in Have a Go* and, to wind up the evening, *Sydney Lipton and his Orchestra.*

A TYPICAL THIRD PROGRAMME SCHEDULE

This schedule is taken from January 1948:

6 p.m. The Dorian Singers
6.30 p.m. The Economic Situation of the USSR
6.50 p.m. Scriabin
7.15 p.m. Arthur Machen
7.35 p.m. Nineteenth-century Broadsheets and Ballads
8.05 p.m. Eighteenth-century Chamber Music
8.50 p.m. Dangerous Drugs: A Study of a Drug Addict
9.50 p.m. Brahms
10.35 p.m.–10.55 p.m. Max Plowman

The Third Programme wasn't without its difficulties. On the one hand, it was seen by some as an essential voice for the arts, and certainly there was a distinguished line-up of contributors, including Benjamin Britten, Samuel Beckett and Philip Larkin. Others saw it as too elitist, but whatever the arguments, there was a rumpus when the biggest shake-up of BBC radio stations took place in 1967. The Third Programme was absorbed into Radio 3; the Home Service became Radio 4, but taking on much of the spoken word of the 'Third', to many people's disgust; the Light Programme became Radio 2; and there was a new pop station, Radio 1.

RADIO 3

Between 90 and 93 FM

In the first couple of years, Radio 3 didn't just play music – there was sport and educational content, too, with the Music Programme, Sport Service and Third Programme in the '3' mix. By 1970, however, these extra strands were absorbed by other stations and the Radio 3 we know today emerged. It's still a real mix – but of music, and there's plenty of it.

An informative breakfast show, incorporating listener requests and a CD review on Saturday mornings with Andrew McGregor; the Composer of the Week, which focuses on getting to know one composer at a time really well; Through the Night, Essential Classics, The Lunchtime Concert, In Tune, Live in Concert and the popular Jazz Line-up. And you can still hear the spoken word, with Drama on 3, Free Thinking and The Essay.

But, of course, Radio 3 is not the only place you can hear great classical music. Since the early 1990s, it has had a rival...

CLASSIC FM

Between 99.9 and 101.9 FM

The strains of Handel's *Zadok the Priest* heralded the launch of the commercial radio station Classic FM in September 1992, and it's hard to believe it's been around for more than 20 years. Reaction to this new station was mixed, many of the opinion that 'classic' and 'commercial' would never mix. What did they know...?

Classic FM has proved that classical music is accessible for all, with a mix of well-known works coupled with less familiar pieces, light classical music, film scores and chat. The purists may have sniffed at the light content, but it's a formula that works; the station pulls in more than five million listeners every week. Classic FM's *Hall of Fame Top 300* is a favourite over the Easter weekend and the *Smooth Classics* programme every evening is the perfect way to unwind.

On Classic FM, just as on Radio 3, there are always mini-biographies of the composers and background information on the pieces played – the little snippets which help so much to appreciate what you're listening to.

LET'S FACE THE MUSIC

Face the Music was a BBC TV classical music quiz programme, which ran from 1966 to 1979, with pianist Joseph Cooper at the helm. It evolved from his successful radio programme, *Call the Tune*, which began in 1954. Members of the *Face the Music* panel included Joyce Grenfell, Richard Baker and Robin Ray (the son of comedian Ted Ray), who nearly always knew not only the piece of music he was listening to but could guess the Opus number, too.

Other panelists included journalist Bernard Levin, travel writer and historian John Julius Norwich and David Attenborough, and the guest list read like a musical Who's Who – William Walton, Dudley Moore, Georg Solti and others. The dummy keyboard was a popular round, where Joseph Cooper would play a soundless piano and the panelists had to guess the tune from his hand movements.

STEVE'S MUSIC

Steve Race was a composer and television presenter who chaired many music programmes both on TV and radio, the best known of which was probably the quiz *My Music*. This ran on the radio for many years before a successful run on television.

The regular panelists were usually Frank Muir, Denis Norden, Owen Brannigan and Ian ('The Hippopotamus') Wallace. Opera singer David Franklin and broadcaster John Amis also appeared. The quiz element was often less important than the entertainment value, especially as each member had to sing a song at the end of the programme, some more successfully than others.

TV AND RADIO THEMES

Television and radio has always had its share of good theme tunes. Between 1950 and 1982, young listeners would tune in to *Listen with Mother*, the well-known theme music being the Berceuse from Fauré's *Dolly Suite*, which was a collection of pieces for two pianists.

Instantly recognisable is the theme tune to *Desert Island Discs* – Eric Coates' 'By the Sleepy Lagoon' – which has been used since the first transmission in 1942 and is still going strong today.

Remember the BBC's *Dr Finlay's Casebook*? Based on the books by A. J. Cronin, the series ran from 1962 to 1972. Many people will be able to hum the tune – but can you name it? It was the 'March' from *A Little Suite*, composed by Trevor Duncan, who worked at the BBC as a sound engineer. He was particularly known for his light music, including the pizzicato 'High Heels', and the sweeping strings of 'The Girl from Corsica', the theme tune to the BBC's Francis Durbridge thriller, *The Scarf*.

The BBC's *Panorama* theme tune sounds as if it should be from a classical piece but it comes from the soundtrack of the film *Un Homme et une Femme*, composed by Francis Lai. This tune was used from the mid 1960s and *Panorama* still uses it today, although it's been brought up-to-date several times. Previous to this (and from the first transmission in 1953) an extract from Jean Sibelius' *Pelléas and Mélisande* was used. The *Mastermind* theme is another one which has a classical weight but is an incidental piece, entitled 'Approaching Menace' (very apt, given the black chair which awaits) and written by the British composer Neil Richardson.

FOR THE LITTLE ONES

Children's programmes have kicked up a surprising amount of classical themes. *Tales of the Riverbank* was a children's BBC series in the sixties and seventies, with Johnny Morris providing the voices for Hammy Hamster, Roderick the Rat and G. P. the guinea pig. The charming guitar music Andante in C by Italian composer and guitar virtuoso Mauro Giuliani (1781–1829) provided the theme music.

In the 1950s, *Picture Book*, which was broadcasted every Monday, was heralded by the sparkling flute of the Badinerie, the final movement of Bach's Orchestral Suite No. 2 in B Minor.

THE POWER OF ADVERTISING

Dreaded adverts: intrusive and unwelcome. Advertisers know this and have used classical music very cleverly over the years to wean us from nipping to the loo or putting the kettle on during a break.

Remember the Hamlet cigar advert? The unseen golfer gouging up sand as he tries to hit the ball out of the bunker, then, giving up, the sound of a match and the first puff of cigar smoke wafting up into the air to the strains of Bach's 'Air on the G String'. Relax with Bach…

And do you recall when everyone went mad for a certain nutty, fruity chocolate bar? Frank Muir told us all about the delightful confectionary to the tune of 'Dance of the Mirlitons' from Tchaikovsky's ballet *The Nutcracker*.

A little more exotic was the hunky surfer riding the Old Spice waves to the tune of Carl Orff's 'O Fortuna' from the opera

Carmina Burana (with the obligatory *femme fatale* wafting her hair about).

And you could take to the skies with British Airways and Léo Delibes... several versions of the flower duet from his opera *Lakmé* graced their adverts and somehow the combination of the soaring melody and colourful snapshots of exotic locations was exactly right. Clever advertising...

And what about the little boy with his bike struggling up a hill, his basket laden with brown bread? This 1973 Hovis advert, directed by *Blade Runner*, *Alien* and *Gladiator* director, Ridley Scott, was to the strains of the second movement of Antonín Dvořák's Symphony No. 9, 'From the New World'.

Finally, what better way to accompany that morning cup of Nescafé coffee than by playing 'Morning Mood' from *Peer Gynt* by Edvard Grieg. Incidentally, the music was penned to accompany Ibsen's play of the same name – a labour of love, apparently, as Grieg said he found the play a 'terribly unmanageable subject' to set to music.

SHOWING AT YOUR LOCAL CINEMA

There are films galore that have classical references, music or themes.

Dudley Moore's character had everything in the 1979 film *10*, but he wanted more, in particular the beaded and unattainable Bo Derek. The film charts his mid-life crisis to the strains of Ravel's *Boléro* and Prokofiev's *Romeo and Juliet*.

The helicopters flying into battle to Wagner's 'Ride of the Valkyries' in *Apocalypse Now* is a stunning use of classical music.

Ken Russell's 1970 film *The Music Lovers* featured Richard Chamberlain as the tortured Tchaikovsky; one of several films he made about classical composers, which are all worth a watch if you like Russell's interpretations.

The 2012 film *Quartet* stars Tom Courtenay, Maggie Smith, Billy Connolly and Pauline Collins as opera singers who live in a home for retired musicians, and marked Dustin Hoffman's directorial debut. What was refreshing was that (the main characters apart) the 'residents' in the film could actually play their instruments, having been members of orchestras.

Movies for younger viewers often use classical music to good effect too. 'The Carol of the Bells', based on a Ukrainian folk song, goes at a lick and is marvellous for breath control if you're a singer. You'll have heard it in the films *Home Alone* and *Harry Potter and the Prisoner of Azkaban*.

Film footnotes...

o William Walton's score for *Battle of Britain* (1969)

o Richard Strauss' 'Also Sprach Zarathustra' in the film *2001: A Space Odyssey* (1968)

o Samuel Barber's Adagio for Strings in *Platoon* (1986)

o Ennio Morricone's 'Gabriel's Oboe' theme in *The Mission* (1986)

o Erik Satie's Gnossienne No. 1 in *Chocolat* (2000)

o Jacques Offenbach's 'Infernal Galop' (otherwise known as the 'Can Can'), from his opera *Orpheus in the Underworld*, in Baz Luhrmann's film *Moulin Rouge!* (2001)

o Mahler's Symphony No. 5, fourth movement, 'Adagietto', in the film *Death in Venice* (1971)

o Handel's *Music for the Royal Fireworks* and *Zadok the Priest* in *The Madness of King George* (1994)

o Mozart's String Quintet No. 6 in E-flat major, K614, in *When Harry Met Sally...* (1989)

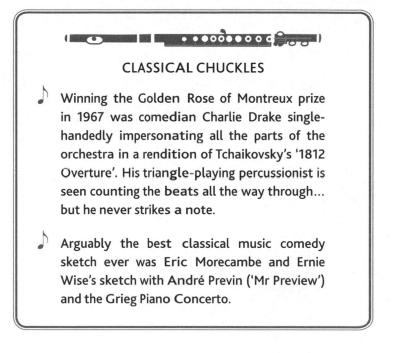

CLASSICAL CHUCKLES

♪ Winning the Golden Rose of Montreux prize in 1967 was comedian Charlie Drake single-handedly impersonating all the parts of the orchestra in a rendition of Tchaikovsky's '1812 Overture'. His triangle-playing percussionist is seen counting the beats all the way through... but he never strikes a note.

♪ Arguably the best classical music comedy sketch ever was Eric Morecambe and Ernie Wise's sketch with André Previn ('Mr Preview') and the Grieg Piano Concerto.

A MUSICAL MISCELLANY

THE FESTIVE SEASON

Christmas is a time for midnight services, goodwill to all men and the Queen's speech. But it's also a time for those who would never normally flex their voice muscles to clear their throats and sing a carol or two.

THE CHRISTMAS CAROL: HOW IT ALL BEGAN

After the pre-Christmas frenzy of writing out cards, shopping for presents, ordering the turkey and stocking the fridge with food, there's one thing that makes the Christmas season complete; to listen to a Christmas carol or two – and not those you hear endlessly looped in supermarkets.

Listening to or singing those well-loved tunes gives us the opportunity to take stock of what Christmas is all about – be it a carol concert at church, village hall or school, listening to carol singers at the door or watching the service of Nine Lessons and

Carols which has been broadcast from King's College Chapel, in Cambridge, every Christmas Eve since 1928.

But have you ever wondered about how the Christmas carol came to be? The first carols had little to do with Christmas and were sung at any time of the year, being written for celebrations and special occasions, as the word 'carol' translates as 'song of joy'. Pagan songs were sung in Europe to celebrate the winter solstice and the feast of Yule (which became Christmastide).

This didn't impress the early Christian Church, the outcome of its struggle on the subject with 'pagan' man being that if they must sing songs, they had to be of a religious nature. Early compositions celebrating the birth of Christ were in Latin and were not carols, as such, but hymns.

The fourth-century Saint Hilary of Poitiers wrote one of the earliest known Christmas hymns – 'Jesus Refulsit Omnium' ('Jesus, Light of All the Nations'). He was Bishop of Poitiers and some regard him as the first Latin Christian hymn-writer. (Hilary term at Oxford University is so named because Saint Hilary's feast day, 14 January, falls during this term.)

History credits Saint Francis of Assisi with introducing the Christmas tradition of carolling in the 1200s (before this time, congregations had to sit and listen to the priests singing Christmas hymns). He's also credited with setting up the first nativity scene in 1223. In late-medieval Italy, the *lauda* – a folk song associated with Christmas – put in an appearance. It was the equivalent of the English carol and was often sung by roaming troubadours.

It wasn't until the fifteenth century, in 1426, that the first recorded carols written in English, by John Audelay, a chaplain from Shropshire, emerged. His collection of Christmas carols bore the following inscription:

> *'I pray you, sirs, both more and less,*
> *Sing these carols in Christmas.'*

It could be that Audelay's carols were in fact wassailing songs (the boundaries, as with the *lauda,* being somewhat blurred) and sung door-to-door by wassailers, the forerunners of carolers today.

The origins of wassailing can be traced back to Anglo-Saxon times, the word 'wassail' coming from the toast, *weas hael,* meaning 'good health'. The wassail cup of hot mulled cider and spices would be drunk, generally on the twelfth night after Christmas, to toast a good apple harvest.

The Protestant Martin Luther encouraged the singing of carols in church services; Oliver Cromwell and his Puritan cronies, however, put a stop to all Christmas celebrations, barely 100 years later (around 1650). It wasn't until the 1800s that the Christmas carol properly resurfaced, with the publication of William Sandys' collection of carols, *Christmas Carols Ancient and Modern*: the Victorians' revival of the Christmas carol had begun. Christmas carols remain an important part of our worship and celebration today, their history as fascinating as they are tuneful.

- 'Personent Hodie' is considered to be one of the earliest carols (as opposed to a hymn), and was originally published in 1582 in a volume of medieval Finnish songs, *Piae Cantiones,* with Latin texts collected by a Lutheran cleric. A similar melody had been found in a 1360 manuscript in Germany and it is from this manuscript that the song is usually dated. It tells of the joy of the Christmas message, the lowliness of Christ's birth, the Wise Men following the star and praises given to the new King.

- 'Adam Lay Ybounden' may well have started life as either a lyrical song or for use in a mystery play – either way, the words, in Middle English, date back to the fifteenth century. Listen to Benjamin Britten's *A Ceremony of Carols* for a rip-roaring interpretation, or composer Basil Ord's version which is a beautiful meld of four-part harmony.

o Stop reading now if you're squeamish because 'The Boar's Head Carol', yes, does indeed concern a boar's head.

> *'Bedecked with bay and rosemary, I pray you,*
> *my masters, be merry... The boar's head, as I*
> *understand, is the bravest dish in all the land.'*

This carol harks back to the ancient ceremony of serving up a boar's head at a Yuletide feast, and a tradition which Queen's College, Oxford, performed on Christmas Eve for many years.

o The authorship of 'O Come, All Ye Faithful' ('Adeste Fideles') is uncertain, though it has been attributed to the Catholic John Francis Wade, who fled to France after the Jacobite rising in 1745. It's rather sad that we know so little about one of our best-loved carols.

o 'Hark! The Herald Angels Sing' didn't start out as quite the carol we know today. It was originally set to a rather slow and sombre tune (not the one that is sung now) and the words were written by Methodist preacher Charles Wesley in 1739 as 'Hark! How all the welkin [heaven] rings, Glory to the King of Kings'. These words were changed over the years and Felix Mendelssohn composed a new tune, which was a great and enduring success.

o One of our best-loved carols, 'Silent Night' ('Stille Nacht'), has Austrian heritage. The words were written by priest Joseph Mohr, and the melody and guitar accompaniment was composed by schoolteacher Franz Gruber in 1818. It was first performed on Christmas Eve of that year; why a guitar was used is not certain, but it has been suggested that it was because the organ was out of action. Whatever the story, the carol has resonated over the years, not least on Christmas Eve, 1914, when English and German soldiers laid down their arms to sing the carol.

o The words of 'In the Bleak Midwinter' are from a poem by Christina Rossetti. It has proved quite difficult to set the words to music as the metre is irregular, and there are extra syllables all over the place, for example, '**Our God**, Heaven cannot hold him' and '**Heaven and earth** shall flee **away**'. However, it didn't stop either Gustav Holst or Harold Darke setting the poem to music. Holst's tune, Cranham, probably just tips the scales as being slightly better known, but Darke's tune has the darker feel to it.

A FESTIVAL OF NINE LESSONS AND CAROLS

For many people, Christmas Eve just wouldn't be the same without listening to this service from King's College Chapel, Cambridge. It was first held in 1918 to foster a more creative approach to worship, and it worked, as it is now broadcast every year to millions of people around the world. The opening carol is always 'Once in Royal David's City' and every year there is a specially commissioned carol.

GRACE NOTE

The tune of the German carol 'O Christmas Tree' ('O Tannenbaum') comes from a sixteenth-century folk song, and is also used as the tune of 'The Red Flag', the song associated with left-wing politics and which has been sung at the end of Labour party conferences since 1925.

CLASSICAL CHUCKLES

How many folk singers does it take to change a light bulb?

One to change it and five to sing about how good the old one was.

WE'RE GOING LIVE

Even with the best technology that is used to broadcast radio or television concerts, there's simply nothing like live music. Finding your seat, the buzz of the audience, the sense of anticipation when the curtain rises or the conductor walks to the podium...

THE VIENNA NEW YEAR'S CONCERT

After the carol concerts, the Nine Lessons and Carols from King's College, Cambridge, and the general winding down of the festive season, there's a brief period of stillness before the New Year's celebrations begin.

Vienna has become synonymous with bringing in the New Year in style, and just one of the events it hosts is the Vienna Philharmonic's New Year's Day Concert, which is broadcast from the Musikverein to countries around the world.

There are always works by Strauss and other Austrian composers, so you'll hear plenty of polkas, mazurkas and waltzes. Up until 1980, the concert was always led by an Austrian conductor, but now there's a guest conductor every year. Herbert von Karajan, Nikolaus Harnoncourt, Claudio Abbado, Daniel Barenboim and Riccardo Muti have all taken a turn, so you'll know you're in for a treat if you tune in on New Year's Eve.

THE BBC PROMS

The promenade concerts in London are a great introduction to the world of classical music, as there's always so much choice during the eight-week season of concerts that run in the summer – there's bound to be a programme that will fit the bill.

A STROLL IN THE PARK

They're called promenade concerts because that's what the well-heeled members of society did years ago – strolled around what were known as pleasure gardens, listening to music. In the late 1700s and early 1800s, it was the thing to be seen at Ranelagh Gardens in Chelsea or Vauxhall Gardens in Kennington, where gentry and royalty met for firework displays, concerts, social chit-chat over supper, and probably for naughty assignations, too. And all for an admission price of around three shillings.

Of course, the tradition of listening to music in the open air during the summer months is still going strong, with Battle Proms picnic concerts, Proms Spectacular and countrywide summer proms – there's sure to be a concert on somewhere nearby, just don't forget to wear your thermals, and take a cushion and an umbrella.

SIR HENRY AND ALL THAT

The origins of what would become the BBC Proms go back to August 1895 when Robert Newman, manager of the Queen's Hall in London, wanted to put on concerts which would attract people who wouldn't normally think of going to hear classical music. The informal atmosphere and the low ticket prices achieved just that.

He offered the post of conductor to Henry Wood, complete with a permanent orchestra at Queen's Hall. Wood and Newman were keen to introduce audiences to a wide-ranging mix of music, including new works every prom season, but with plenty of familiar pieces, too.

By 1927, the BBC took over these Proms, with Henry Wood and his symphony orchestra still at the helm, until the BBC Symphony Orchestra was formed in 1930. With the outbreak of war, however, the BBC withdrew its support yet the Proms continued regardless. When the Queen's Hall was destroyed by bombing in May 1941, the Proms moved to its current venue, the Royal Albert Hall, with the BBC again becoming involved. Henry Wood continued in his role until he died in 1944, just short of completing 50 years as Proms' conductor.

Adrian Boult and Malcolm Sargent are the two best-remembered post-war conductors – not least for the dapper, carnation-buttonholed Sargent's witty chiding of the 'Prommers' (those potentially rowdy members of the audience who stand in the arena or gallery areas), telling them to behave.

And so the Proms continue, with other venues now, too, although the Albert Hall is still the home of the main concerts; and there's still so much for everyone to enjoy – lunchtime concerts, children's Proms, Proms in the Park, and for some years, there was even a Blue Peter Prom, not to mention a Doctor Who-themed Prom.

The mixed bag of music is still the same – from Mozart to Messiaen, Wagner to Walton (with music from *Mary Poppins* and Ron Grainer in there somewhere, too). To this day, the Proms strives to play accessible music for all in order to ensure the tradition continues – Robert Newman and Henry Wood would undoubtedly approve.

THE LAST NIGHT

The real attraction for many people is to attend Last Night of the Proms, especially to go as a 'Prommer', which is an option for any enthusiast because ticket prices are ridiculously cheap – at present a steal at £5 each. Prommers come armed with streamers, balloons, party poppers and Union Jacks, and there's a real party atmosphere, especially when time-honoured pieces, such as Elgar's *Pomp and Circumstance*, 'Land of Hope and Glory', and 'Rule, Britannia!', are played.

HANDY HINTS FOR PROMMERS

o Take bottled water – it gets very hot

o You'll be standing, so comfortable footwear is essential

o Don't talk or open crisp packets in the quiet bits

o Do remember to shout 'Heave!' when the grand piano lid is lifted up

o Do clap when the piano note is played for the orchestra to tune up

o Silly hats and accoutrements for the last night only, please – you'll look pretty daft if you turn up in fancy dress for Bach's B Minor Mass

AND TALKING OF SILLY

Orchestras and conductors have had their moments on the last night, too. For instance, a prom in 2009 featured the English composer Malcolm Arnold's 'A Grand, Grand Overture', which starred an orchestra, a floor polisher (AKA David Attenborough), three vacuums and four shotguns. It had been commissioned for a series of musical festivals which cartoonist Gerard Hoffnung created in the late 1950s. 'A Grand, Grand Overture' has a grand, grand finale à la Beethoven, with chords that go on forever. Great fun!

THE THREE (TOP) Gs

GLYNDEBOURNE

If you fancy a bit of operatic culture, then Glyndebourne, near Lewes in East Sussex, is the place to be in the summer. Founded in 1934, the Glyndebourne Opera Festival runs every year from May to August. There is no dress code, so evening dress is not obligatory, but it is customary (and all part of the Glyndebourne fun) to get togged up. It's an all-day experience, consisting of a picnic on the lawns overlooking the South Downs, then into the theatre to hear the opera. The productions are first class – always an eclectic mix of composers and eras – and Glyndebourne has a reputation for being expert in the Mozart department.

GARSINGTON

Garsington Opera has been going since 1989 and started out at Garsington Manor, near Oxford, until circumstances necessitated a move to the Wormsley Estate, 15 miles down the road. It's still just as enchanting an experience; the Chilterns beyond, lovely views of the gardens from the auditorium, and you can picnic or quaff champagne in the opera pavilion – plus there's opera, and lots of it! The season runs in June and July, and includes Mozart and Rossini, as well as other new productions.

GRANGE PARK

The new kid on the block, founded in 1998, is Grange Park Opera, situated in Hampshire at the neo-classical mansion The Grange between Basingstoke and Winchester. The theatre is sited in the orangery, where four operas feature over a six-week summer season. Past productions include *Iolanthe*, *The Cunning Little Vixen*, *The Magic Flute* and *Idomeneo*. Dinner, afternoon tea or a picnic; the choice is yours, but all can be experienced in pleasant surroundings.

YOU'RE UP NEXT: COMPETITIONS

Music competitions never fail to surprise and delight – there is always such a prodigious amount of young musical talent. It is also a source of wonder that not only do these young people put in hours of dedicated practice, but they remain calm, composed and supremely confident under the most intense pressure. Competitions have produced consummate artists, such as violinist Nicola Benedetti and clarinettist Emma Johnson, both of whom have gone on to forge hugely successful careers.

BBC CARDIFF SINGER OF THE WORLD

This competition is held biannually and was started in 1983 to commemorate the opening of St David's Hall in Cardiff. The competition has launched the careers of successful singers including bass-baritone Bryn Terfel and Finnish soprano Karita Mattila.

BBC YOUNG MUSICIAN OF THE YEAR

Eighteen-year-old pianist Martin James Bartlett won this competition in 2014 with, among other pieces, Rachmaninoff's *Rhapsody on the Theme of Paganini*. What's great about the young musician contest is the diverse variety of instruments you hear – from recorders to saxophonists to percussionists. Presented biannually, the show states that all competitors have to be under 18; the youngest winner, trombonist Peter Moore, was only 12 when he won in 2008.

LEEDS INTERNATIONAL PIANO COMPETITION

Founded in 1961 by pianists Fanny Waterman and Marion Thorpe, this competition has launched the careers of Romanian Radu Lupu, who won in 1969, and the fabulous Mitsuko Uchida, who was a finalist in 1975. It's held every three years and competitors enter from around the world. It should come as no surprise then that the standard is absolutely breathtaking.

SURROUND SOUND: THE BEST VENUES

THE ROYAL OPERA HOUSE (ROH) in Bow Street, London, was a dance hall during the Second World War and has a fascinating history which extends back to 1732. It is now an operatic venue that is home to The Royal Opera, The Royal Ballet and the Orchestra of the Royal Opera House. There have been three theatres on the present site, the first two Theatre Royals destroyed by fire, and the third named the Royal Opera House in 1892, but known by many as simply 'Covent Garden'. The auditorium, which seats more than 2,000 people, was lovingly restored to its former glory in 1999. As well as its main repertoire of opera and ballet, it has 'welcome performances', where families can see an opera or ballet at a fraction of the usual ticket price; other events include matinées, dance workshops for schools and teachers' programmes.

LA SCALA, also known as *Teatro alla Scala*, is the world-famous opera house in Milan – another theatre that has had a fiery history, literally. The original building, the Royal Ducal Theatre, was destroyed by a fire in 1776, and the costs of building the new theatre were borne by the owners of the private boxes at the Ducal. Rossini's *La Pietra del Paragone* (*The Touchstone*) was his first commission for a major opera, and its performance at La Scala in 1812 put both composer and opera house on the map. Arturo Toscanini was one of a string of distinguished La Scala musical directors, and the finest artists in the world have performed there, including sopranos Maria Callas and Joan Sutherland, and ballerina Margot Fonteyn. The audiences have the reputation for being the most critical in the world.

SYDNEY OPERA HOUSE opened in 1973, its iconic shape in Sydney Harbour instantly recognisable. The main concert hall is part of a complex of three theatres, a theatre studio and a recording studio, which makes it one of the busiest performing arts centres in the world. It has four in-house companies – Opera Australia, The Australian Ballet, the Sydney Theatre Company and the Sydney Symphony Orchestra. There are 40 shows a week at the Sydney Opera House – including opera, dance, music, circus, theatre and talks on many subjects.

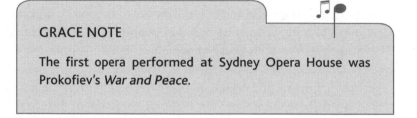

GRACE NOTE

The first opera performed at Sydney Opera House was Prokofiev's *War and Peace.*

THE ROYAL FESTIVAL HALL (RFH) has been around since 1951, when it was opened as part of the Festival of Britain. It sits within the Southbank Centre alongside the Queen Elizabeth Hall, the Purcell Room, the Hayward Gallery and the Saison Poetry Library. The RFH underwent substantial renovation in 2007 and, following a huge fundraising campaign, the hall's organ was restored and reinstalled between 2011 and 2013 – all 7,866 pipes of it.

The RFH has three resident orchestras, so when you're visiting London, it's well worth finding out what's on there – and the walk across the Thames over the Hungerford Bridge and Golden Jubilee Bridges to the hall is all part of the experience.

If you want to make it in the USA, then performing in **CARNEGIE HALL** in New York (just two blocks away from Central Park) will tell the world you're a pretty special musician. Carnegie Hall was the brainchild of industrialist Andrew Carnegie who bought the land and built the Hall, which opened in 1891.

What makes it special is that it's not just a venue for classical artists; the world of jazz and popular music is well represented here, too. Mahler, Stokowski, Callas and Toscanini have all performed here – Rachmaninoff made his Carnegie debut in 1909 and Stravinsky in 1925, but so did Benny Goodman's swing orchestra in 1938 and Judy Garland in 1961. So, if you're in New York, and you want to hear anything from Thomas Tallis to *West Side Story*, then pay a visit to Carnegie.

Visit **THE LINCOLN CENTRE** in New York and you'll hear the finest performers and orchestras in the classical music world, including the Metropolitan Opera.

The 'Met' Opera was founded in 1880, its home the Metropolitan Opera House then situated on Broadway at 39th Street. That was until 1966, when they upped sticks and moved to The Lincoln Centre, and the company is now resident there, along with the New York City Ballet, the New York Philharmonic and the famous Juilliard School. The Lincoln Centre, being one of the world's leading performing-arts centres, hosts anything from jazz to chamber music to films. An art lover's heaven.

MUSICAL TEAMWORK

Two in harmony, a terrific trio or a fantastic foursome – describe them how you will, it's not always soloists who have made a musical impression on audiences.

WILLIAM SCHWENCK GILBERT (1836–1911) AND ARTHUR SULLIVAN (1842–1900)

William Gilbert and Arthur Sullivan were both born in London. Their first operatic collaboration, *Thespis*, was not the greatest of successes – under-rehearsed and too long, said the critics. It's a good job that the duo was not discouraged by this dismal start (although they did go their separate ways for three years after *Thespis*), because their next operetta, *Trial by Jury*, was a triumph. Thus began the most successful partnership of wordsmith, Gilbert, and composer, Sullivan, with their comic operas. *Trial by Jury* was the first of the Savoy operas, produced mostly at the Savoy Theatre in London. Others included *HMS Pinafore*, *The Mikado*, *Iolanthe* and *The Pirates of Penzance*. Gilbert's witty words and Sullivan's sense of musical parody have ensured that the operettas, resounding successes then, are still just as popular today.

GRACE NOTE

If you haven't seen the 1999 Mike Leigh film *Topsy-Turvy* with Jim Broadbent as Gilbert and Allan Corduner as Sullivan then you've missed a treat. Thoroughly recommended.

MARJAN RAWICZ (1898–1970)
AND WALTER LANDAUER (1910–1983)

A popular piano duo that met by chance in Austria when Landauer heard Rawicz whistling a tune and asked him to play it on the piano. So started a career lasting 40 years, from the 1930s to the 1970s. They moved with their wives to the UK, but were interned on the Isle of Man as possible 'enemies of the people' during World War Two. On their release, they became British subjects. Renowned for their precision-playing of popular classics, they made many BBC broadcasts and became a favourite of Charles, Prince of Wales. Upon Rawicz's death, Landauer continued as a solo artist.

AMADEUS QUARTET

Probably the most famous string foursome in the world. Founded in 1947, the quartet was remarkable in that it retained its four original players throughout its 40-year history, disbanding only with the death of its viola player, Peter Schidlof. The quartet made around 200 recordings, including the complete quartets of Mozart and Beethoven.

MICHAEL FLANDERS (1922–75)
AND DONALD SWANN (1923–94)

The musical comedy duo, they of the 'A Transport of Delight' song, performed their *At the Drop of a Hat* revues for 11 years. As a result of polio, singer Michael Flanders was confined to a wheelchair, so with Donald Swann, the pianist, they both performed sitting down.

They wrote a huge number of comedy songs (some produced on disc by The Beatles' producer, George Martin) including 'In the D'Oyly Cart' and 'Ill Wind', based on the rondo of Mozart's Horn Concerto No. 4 in E-flat Major.

THE THREE TENORS

Plácido Domingo (b.1941)
Luciano Pavarotti (1935–2007)
José Carreras (b.1946)

The performances of The Three Tenors have passed into legend. Although the three singers have had hugely successful careers as individuals, and even though sadly Pavarotti died in 2007, whenever one of their names is mentioned, the other two are not far behind in the telling. Yet the story of how The Three Tenors came to sing together is probably not generally known.

It was the idea of José Carreras who, on hearing that plans for a special concert were afoot for the 1990 World Cup, suggested that the three best tenors in the world sing: José Carreras, Luciano Pavarotti and Plácido Domingo.

The world took the three to its heart – that concert on the eve of the World Cup, which raised money for Carreras' Leukaemia Foundation, was the first of many more collaborations. The world tours and benefit concerts were a huge success and brought classical music to a much wider audience than if they performed at an opera house or a concert hall. They gave their last Three Tenors' performance in 2003.

MUSIC, MUSIC, MUSIC: THEATRICAL SCORES

If you're not familiar with opera, it may all seem a little highbrow. But go to one and you'll be absorbed in scandal and controversy, be it Carmen giving it her lustful all, Don Giovanni having a dust up with the devil or ladies succumbing to the vapours and worse on sofas... If you aren't so much interested in the storyline, the overtures to many operas are pretty impressive too.

OPERAS

Princess Margaret once described opera as 'fat people shouting at each other'. Not to disagree with Royalty, but...

DON GIOVANNI, MOZART

Lust, seduction, revenge, danger, and a bit of comedy thrown in for good measure. Will womaniser Don Giovanni repent of his sins? Based on the story of Don Juan, Mozart's music is every bit as dramatic. There's a great duet, 'Là ci darem la mano' ('Give me thy hand, oh fairest'), when Don Giovanni is at his seductive best, and the climax when Giovanni receives his comeuppance and is taken down into hell is a real thrill.

THE MAGIC FLUTE, MOZART

After the dramatic opening phrases of the first minute and a half, in come those strings stirring up a storm. We have Papageno the bird catcher, the Queen of the Night (whose almost Wagnerian aria goes so high the notes enter the stratosphere!), her daughter, Pamina, and Sarastro the Sorcerer. This high-octane Mozartian fantasy-fling is made all the more remarkable with the knowledge that he wrote it in his final year and it was premiered only three months before he died.

LA TRAVIATA, VERDI

After a less than promising debut in 1853 (for a start, the soprano who played the consumptive Violetta was more than adequately 'rounded'), this has become one of the most popular operas of all time. Violetta is a courtesan, who loves Alfredo, but his father has other ideas about the liaison – it can only lead to misunderstanding and tragedy. Listen out for the 'Drinking Song' in act one and the massive duet between Violetta and Alfredo's father in act two.

LA BOHÈME, PUCCINI

Another consumptive heroine – poor old Mimi (she of the cold hands) is in love with Rodolfo but they are doomed. This opera has an unmatched emotional intensity and three of the finest arias you will hear: Rodolfo's 'Che gelida manina' ('Your tiny hand is frozen'), Mimi's stunning 'Mi chiamano Mimi' ('They call me Mimi') and their final song together before Mimi dies, 'Sono andati?' ('Have they gone?'). Have the tissues handy.

GRACE NOTE

Scott Joplin (c.1867/8–1917), dubbed 'The King of Ragtime', is famous for the songs 'Maple Leaf Rag', 'The Entertainer' and 'Easy Winners' – but you may not know that he wrote the opera *Treemonisha*. He actually wrote two operas but the first, *A Guest of Honor* [sic], was lost when a touring production of the opera ran into financial trouble in 1903 and Joplin was forced to leave behind a trunk of belongings. In it was the score to *A Guest of Honor*, which is now presumed to be lost. *Treemonisha* is not a ragtime opera, although there are many syncopated rhythms and jazz influences the finale, A Real Slow Drag, is a stirring end. If you like his rags, try Antoinette and also Fig Leaf Rag.

CARMEN, BIZET

This Carmen is hot stuff; the opera's racy plot with Don José and bullfighter Escamillo both after the fiery Carmen scandalised audiences on its premiere, the critics being none too kind, either – well, it was 1875. But it's great stuff; as Carmen keeps both men dangling, her feminine wiles getting her out of trouble on more than one occasion. You'll probably know the 'Toreador Song' and Carmen's 'L'amour est un oiseau rebelle' ('Love is a rebellious bird'). Naughty but nice.

THE BARBER OF SEVILLE, ROSSINI

Like *Carmen*, this comic opera took a while to sink in with audiences – actually that's a bit of an understatement; the first performance in 1816 was a disaster, probably more to do with composer rivalry than the quality of the opera. But it was soon a favourite, and still is. Romance and resourcefulness are what it's all about – the Count loves Rosina but her doddery old guardian has also got his beady eyes on her. Enter Figaro the barber, who devises all sorts of ways to bring the lovers together... The opera has a real energy about it, and there's the great tongue-twisting aria from Figaro himself.

MADAME BUTTERFLY, PUCCINI

This is one of the saddest and most moving operas of all – the tale of hope, despair and betrayal. The young Butterfly marries American naval officer Pinkerton, but he has to leave and she waits patiently with the little boy she bore him. After three years of hope, looking daily for his ship to sail into harbour, he comes back but he's not alone – he returns with a wife – and there is a tragic ending. This opera is a moving juxtaposition of a tale of cruelty combined with the most beautiful music and superlative arias, including 'Un Bel Di' ('One Fine Day') and the duet between Pinkerton and Butterfly, 'Bimba, bimba, non piangere' ('Sweetheart, sweetheart, do not weep'). You will – buckets.

KING HARALD'S SAGA, WEIR

Master of the Queen's Music, Judith Weir wrote this three-act opera based on the Norwegian invasion of England in 1066. It's scored for a solo soprano who sings eight roles, as well as the part of the Norwegian army. No section lasts more than one minute, it's unaccompanied and the whole opera lasts for less than 10 minutes.

PACIFIC OVERTURES, SONDHEIM/WEIDMAN

An opera with a difference; it's really a cross between an opera and a musical but loses nothing of its 'classical' feel for all that. It follows the slow but inevitable westernisation of Japan, from the arrival of the Four Black Dragons (warships arriving in the harbour) to the finale song 'Next', as the country moves from one commercial innovation to the next. The sailors' trio 'Pretty Lady' is hauntingly lovely.

GRACE NOTE

The world's shortest opera is believed to be *Sands of Time* by Welsh composer Peter Reynolds, with the libretto by Simon Rees. The story of Flo and Stan, who win the pools, lasts 3 minutes and 43 seconds. There's a hint of Mozart and a nod to Gilbert and Sullivan in there. Great fun!

Reynolds' opera knocked Darius Milhaud's 1927 *The Deliverance of Theseus* off the top spot, which could be sung in 7 minutes and 27 seconds.

OVERTURES

THE MARRIAGE OF FIGARO, MOZART

Full of brio and *joie de vivre*, this four-minute presto overture sets the scene for one of Mozart's most popular operas, written in 1786. It's been played in any number of films, including the musical door lock to Willy Wonka's chocolate room in the Gene Wilder version of *Willy Wonka and the Chocolate Factory*.

'1812 OVERTURE', TCHAIKOVSKY

If sound effects, derring-do and a whole lot of (musical!) noise is your thing then the '1812 Overture', complete with cannon, will do very well. Tchaikovsky wrote the piece to commemorate Russia's defence against Napoleon. His melancholy, tortured persona has been well-documented and, who knows, maybe this piece was a way of letting off steam, although it is said he took no delight in this 'loud and noisy' overture.

WILLIAM TELL OVERTURE, ROSSINI

Somebody once said that the definition of an intellectual is someone who can listen to the *William Tell* overture and not think of *The Lone Ranger*. What you may not know, though, is that the extract that everyone recognises is really the finale of the overture, the last of the four little sections: Prelude, Dawn; Storm; Ranz des Vaches; and the finale, March of the Swiss Soldiers (or, as it is more commonly known, *The Lone Ranger* music). In the storm section you can hear the first drops of rain in the woodwinds, the brass instruments representing the height of the storm later on.

THE THIEVING MAGPIE OVERTURE, ROSSINI

He was good, this Rossini – the story goes that the producer of the opera had to lock Rossini in a room the day before the opera opened in order to get him to write the overture, and he threw the music out of the window sheet by sheet for his copyists to orchestrate. He may have written it in 24 hours but it's a stirring start to the opera, which Rossini wrote in 1817. The overture begins with a drum roll – listen out for the delightful magpie chirruping melody in the woodwind. The whole thing is as smooth as syrup three-beats-in-a-bar, and it goes from the major to the minor key, then back to the major again.

TANNHÄUSER OVERTURE, WAGNER

This is an epic overture to go with an epic opera – it builds so slowly that there is a sense of willing it onwards until it's a relief when the brass come in with such beautiful chords, the strings providing a semiquaver accompaniment. The overture is full of richness, grandeur and contrasts that build to a repeat of the string/brass theme. And if you like this, try the overture to his opera *Lohengrin*.

'THE FLIGHT OF THE BUMBLEBEE', RIMSKY-KORSAKOV

Written in 1889, this dizzyingly fast musical interlude (from the composer's opera *The Tale of Tsar Saltan*) captures the buzz and the dart of a bee absolutely brilliantly. It's not only a treat for the ears but it is jaw-dropping to watch nimble-fingered flautists, violinists or pianists (it's been arranged for all three instruments) at full pelt. Wonderful.

BALLETS

THE NUTCRACKER, TCHAIKOVSKY

For a delicate counterbalance, the delightful and delicate 'The Dance of the Sugar Plum Fairy' will do very nicely from Tchaikovsky's ballet score music *The Nutcracker*. Written in 1891, the solo comes in act two, and is played by the perfect instrument for the melody line – the bell-like celesta. You won't find better ballet music than Tchaikovsky's.

THE FIREBIRD, STRAVINSKY

This ballet was written in 1910 for impresario Sergei Diaghilev's Ballet Russes. A story of love and magic, the hero Ivan has to overcome the wicked magician Kostcheï and his spells (with the help of the firebird) in order to marry his Princess.

Stravinsky's music is full of drama, fireworks and contrasting moods; the last sections of the ballet are good examples. 'Infernal Dance' has an excitingly loud flurry of strings, brass and woodwind that whips up the magician and his followers to dance until they're exhausted. In the following quiet passage, the bassoon and oboe's haunting question-and-answer themes represent the firebird lulling these characters to sleep. The Princess's musical theme then enters as a horn solo under a layer of long tremulous string notes and the orchestra builds up to a satisfying close with strong brass statements.

MUSIC THROUGH THE AGES: PART FIVE

MODERN TIMES

OLD AND NEW IN HARMONY

There continues to be a wonderfully diverse mix of classical music today – we have the great symphonies, concertos, sonatas and songs that have been played and enjoyed since time immemorial, but we also have innovation in composition, performance and technique.

The instruments of the classical orchestra are still with us, of course, but instrumental and technical boundaries continue to be pushed. For example, Singapore-born classical violinist Vanessa-Mae is well known for using an electric violin in some of her performances and for fusing violin and synthesised sounds to produce new takes on classical music – she's recorded a really funky version of Bach's Toccata and Fugue in D Minor. Computer technology lets us compose our own music any way we want to (stretching and mixing sounds, changing the pitch).

Recommended listening

The rich and complex dissonant densities of American composer Eric Whitacre's music, for instance, are entirely modern but more than a nod to polyphonic chant. His song 'Go, Lovely Rose' is a good example. American composer David Lang's 'The Little Match Girl Passion' is an intriguing work for vocal quartet, full of shifting rhythms and melodies, repetitions of musical phrases and overlapping lines – entirely reminiscent of Renaissance plainchant and yet very twenty-first century.

TUNEFUL TRAILBLAZERS

STRAVINSKY, IGOR (1882-1971)

Stravinsky is known for three distinct styles of music: the Russian works, his neoclassical period and what was known as serial music.

Neoclassical music meant a return to some of the forms of the classical or the baroque era, including balance, clarity and restraint. His 1920 ballet *Pulcinella* is a good example; the music is described as 'after Pergolesi' (Giovanni Battista Pergolesi, the baroque composer) in reference to its restrained style.

Some people were baffled with his return to music styles of the past because his most famous work, the ballet *The Rite of Spring*, with its Russian folk tunes, caused uproar in 1913 because of its savage music score and pounding rhythms, and the dancer Nijinsky's naughty choreography. The roles of the orchestra often switch around, too – for instance the strings take on a pulse beat normally played by the brass, so it was a really innovative work. And obviously outrageous!

But then, in his later years, Stravinsky threw the musical rulebook out of the window again, exploring new serial music using the 12-tone technique devised by Arnold Schoenberg. His 1962 musical play *The Flood* is a good example.

Recommended listening

The dramatic short 1908 orchestral work 'Feu d'Artifice' ('Fireworks') has a flavour of the musical fireworks to come.

PROKOFIEV, SERGEI (1891–1953)

Part-Russian Romantic, part-modern, Sergei Prokofiev was another curious type of composer. The lyrical opening of his Piano Concerto No. 1 in D-flat Major (1912) has a distinctly Rachmaninoff quality to it, but it soon segues into brilliant dissonant melodies and bravura passages which challenge the pianist to the utmost. (His Piano Concerto No. 2 in C Minor is even more difficult.)

Like other Russian composers of the time, his music suffered with the interference of the Soviet authorities, and he spent some years living in America and France, returning to his homeland eventually in 1936, which was a mistake, as this marked the beginning of the Stalinist repressive regime.

But despite the political upheavals, Prokofiev wrote some delightful music – his opera *The Love for Three Oranges* (1919) and the lovely 'Classical' Symphony No. 1 in D Major (1917) have distinctly Mozartian touches, for example. Also his lovely *Romeo and Juliet* that was composed in 1935 but didn't premiere in Russia until 1940 – no doubt the work by this 'degenerate modernist' wasn't fit for Russian ears.

Mention of the name Prokofiev undoubtedly calls to mind his composition *Peter and the Wolf* – a perfect example of how the instruments of the orchestra can be used cleverly to 'paint pictures'; in this case, the animals in a children's story. Unusually Sergei Prokofiev not only wrote the score but also wrote the story, in 1936. Peter is represented by the string section, Grandfather by the bassoon, the bird by the flute, the cat by the clarinet, the wolf by the menacing sound of the French horns, and the duck (who is eaten by the wolf) by the oboe. The story is told as the orchestra plays, and notable narrators have included Eleanor Roosevelt in 1950, Hermione Gingold in 1975 and David Bowie in 1978.

Recommended listening

'Dance of the Knights' from *Romeo and Juliet* is full of drama, the intense string and brass opening theme giving way to a peaceful string and woodwind interlude before the main tune returns with a bang.

SHOSTAKOVICH, DMITRI (1906-75)

Unlike his two fellow countrymen, Prokofiev and Stravinsky, Shostakovich remained in Russia all his life and he really did come up against it. Condemned, on the one hand, as an enemy of the people for his bourgeois music but, on the other, promoted as the Revolution's prodigy, Shostakovich trod a very thin line between producing works that satisfied both the authorities and his own musical longings.

In 1936, Stalin went to a performance of Shostakovich's opera *Lady Macbeth of the Mtsensk District*, which was dubbed 'Muddle instead of Music' and 'coarse' by the *Pravda* newspaper the next day. Realising that his next symphony (his fourth) might also cause dissent, he began to work on a fifth which he described as 'A Soviet artist's response to just criticism'. It did the trick, as it was much more classical in style. But despite the criticisms and having to write 'safe' work, he wrote some stunning music – his seventh symphony is inspired by the siege of Leningrad, and is one of his finest works.

Recommended listening

Violin Concerto No. 1 – written at a time in the late 1940s when repression was at its worst, it wasn't premiered until some years later. It stood as a triumph over repression and was written for the violinist David Oistrach, who asked Shostakovich to put at least a few bars' rest in for the soloist.

COPLAND, AARON (1900-90)

Although *Fanfare for the Common Man* is a cracking piece of music, Copland shouldn't be remembered for just that. Interestingly, there is a very old YouTube clip of him conducting it, and he takes it a lot faster than most versions. What was great about this American composer was that he blended so many styles in his works, including classical, jazz and folk.

New York-born Copland went off to Paris in 1920 to study composition with renowned composer and teacher Nadia Boulanger. It was a heady, creative time for the young man, who was one of a number of young American composers rubbing shoulders with artists, writers and thinkers. Back in America, he wrote his Symphony for Organ and Orchestra, which was debuted in 1925 – it's an intense and mature piece for such a young man, but full of those lovely Copland rhythmic syncopations, brass explosions and percussion quirks that came to blossom in later years.

Musicians found his early works, such as 'Symphonic Ode' (1929), difficult to play and Copland himself realised that his music should be accessible to all. So, he began writing for films, such as *Our Town* (1940), and music for ballet including *Billy the Kid* (1938) and, probably his two best known, *Rodeo* (1942) and *Appalachian Spring* (1944). In 1950, he won an Academy Award for his score for the film *The Heiress*. Although he wrote other perhaps more mainstream works – including a symphony, chamber music for strings, flute and clarinet, and the opera *The Tender Land* (1954) – it is his American period of music for which he's principally remembered.

Recommended listening

The quintet 'The Promise of Living' from *The Tender Land* is the choral finale, and is a simple, melodic hymn to the harvest.

BRITTEN, BENJAMIN (1913–76)

One of the greatest British composers of the twentieth century, Britten had begun composing from an early age in his hometown Lowestoft, in Suffolk. His work attracted the attention of the composer Frank Bridge, who agreed to teach the 14-year-old. After three years at the Royal College of Music, he landed a job with the Post Office film unit, penning the music for various documentaries, including the 1936 film *Night Mail*, in collaboration with the poet W. H. Auden – an association that was to prove important throughout his career.

Britten developed a passion for song cycles and opera, and in 1936, together with Auden, he wrote his first significant song cycle, *Our Hunting Fathers*.

In 1939, Britten and his lifelong partner, tenor Peter Pears, left for the States, returning three years later. It is hard to put a value on the mutually creative musical dynamic that this personal partnership engendered but, certainly from letters to each other, it is clear that they both felt that neither could have achieved what they did alone.

While in America, Britten wrote a number of works, including his large orchestral work *Sinfonia da Requiem,* the operetta *Paul Bunyan* and the first of many song cycles for Pears. Possibly to take his mind off the potentially dangerous wartime sea voyage home, he composed *A Ceremony of Carols* and 'Hymn to St Cecilia' – he'd already started the hymn in the US, but American customs officials had confiscated his music manuscripts, fearing they were codes of some sort.

Back home again in England, Britten began work on his

first great opera, *Peter Grimes* (based on a collection of poems called *The Borough*, by the Suffolk poet George Crabbe), which established Britten beyond any doubt as a twentieth-century musical great. Further operas followed such as *The Rape of Lucretia* (1946) and the comedy *Albert Herring* (1947).

In 1946, Britten founded the English Opera Group and, two years later, the Aldeburgh Festival, writing new works for it nearly every year until his death in 1976. At first the festival was located in local churches and halls but, in 1967, the festival created a permanent home in nearby Snape Maltings. Britten's last opera, *Death in Venice* (which he had written for Peter Pears to sing the role of Gustav von Aschenbach), was first performed there in 1973.

Benjamin Britten's 'Tema Sacher' for solo cello was composed in 1976, as part of a set of variations written by different composers to celebrate Swiss conductor Paul Sacher's birthday. Britten's contribution comes in at just over one minute.

Recommended listening

Britten was committed to writing for amateur musicians and for young people. Whatever your age, if you don't know Britten's work, his *Young Person's Guide to the Orchestra* is a great introduction.

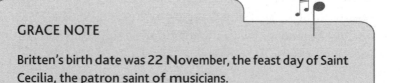

GRACE NOTE

Britten's birth date was 22 November, the feast day of Saint Cecilia, the patron saint of musicians.

BARBER, SAMUEL (1910-81)

This American composer is best known for his sublime Adagio for Strings; it's actually the second movement of his String Quartet in B Minor which he wrote in 1936, and arranged for string orchestra a couple of years later. It's a pity, though, that all we ever seem to hear of Barber on the radio is the Adagio, as he wrote some other pretty good music, too. (The other two movements of the quartet are well worth a listen.)

Early on, Barber planned to make a career as a singer and conductor but, after the success of the Adagio, he concentrated on composing. His 1936 Symphony in One Movement has the broad sweep of film music about it, and really gets stuck in right from the start, while his Violin Concerto is a lyrical pleasure, until he sets off on a rollercoaster last movement. His songs are written with colour and expression; the *Hermit Songs* of the 1950s, based on medieval texts, are quite intense but very tuneful. Mention too should be made of the expressive 'Dover Beach' for string quartet and female voice, and the song 'Music, When Soft Voices Die', which has a simple, lyrical quality and is, musically, very endearing.

Recommended listening

Barber's Symphony in One Movement is dramatic and sprawling with a 'big country' weighty feel – listen for dramatic syncopated chords from the orchestra. It begins with an edgy quality, softened about 12 minutes in with a beautiful oboe solo – a typical Barber melody for those unfamiliar with his work.

GLASS, PHILIP (B.1937)

Philip Glass has always been referred to as one of a group of modern composers noted for their minimalist music, although he has distanced himself from that description by saying that he is a composer of 'music with repetitive structures'. Whatever you might call it; there is no doubt that he has had a huge impact on music of the twentieth and twenty-first centuries. From symphonies to film scores, chamber music to grand opera, his repertoire is broad-ranging and successful; three of his film scores have been nominated for Academy Awards.

After years of struggling to make his way as a composer, his 1976 five-hour opera, *Einstein on the Beach*, is the piece that brought him worldwide recognition. There's neither plot nor narrative, only numbers, syllables, poems and chants, powerful images and dances, and pulsing and reiterating rhythmic patterns. Avant-garde and with no interval, it has been applauded by many critics as a unique and powerful collaborative expression of dance, music and the spoken word.

His 1981 chamber music piece 'Glassworks' also had an impact on a wider audience, and *Orion*, composed in 2004 for his Philip Glass Ensemble, reflects the world's relationship to the heavens as seen by different cultures. He is a composer worth exploring.

Recommended listening

'India' from *Orion* is full of lively rhythms and includes an interesting interweaving of sitar, drums and female vocals.

JENKINS, KARL (B.1944)

Not just classically attuned, but known for his jazz and rock too, Karl Jenkins is the most performed living composer in the world. He began composing classical music later on and is best known for his Mass, *The Armed Man*, and his Requiem.

He started his music career as an oboist in the National Youth Orchestra of Wales, eventually studying at the Royal Academy of Music. For most of his early career, he was known as a jazz musician, playing the saxophone. He joined the rock band Soft Machine in the seventies, and then he began composing music for adverts for which he's won any number of awards.

His series of vocal and orchestral albums, *Adiemus*, took him in a different direction entirely – that of a mix of classical and New Age music – as he experimented with the vocalists singing only sounds, not words, in order to concentrate on the pitch of their voices. The title track 'Adiemus' from the album *Songs of Sanctuary* is instantly recognisable. *The Armed Man* is a work of extraordinary contrasts – compare the sound of marching troops and the imperious brass of the first movement to the soft, almost spiritual violin solo in the Benedictus.

Recommended listening

The Sanctus from *The Armed Man* begins with a soft but powerfully insistent drumbeat, with trumpets and chorus building slowly to a climax with the full orchestra towards the end. The last 30 seconds returns to the first main drumbeat and trumpet theme. It's a sustained and dramatic 7 minutes.

RUTTER, JOHN (B.1945)

Rutter is known chiefly for his choral works and his connection with Cambridge, having read music at Clare College, and being director of music there from 1975 to 1979. In 1981, he formed his own choir, The Cambridge Singers.

Rutter reminisced recently that he was only 18 when David Willcocks looked over some of his work and asked him if he would be interested in seeing any of them published. Would he?! He was amazed and thrilled.

Anthems such as 'A Prayer of St Patrick' and 'God Be in my Head', and longer works such as his Requiem, *Gloria* and *Magnificat* are sung worldwide, as are his Christmas carols. Additionally, he famously co-edited the *Carols for Choirs* series with Willcocks – a staple of songs for choirs countrywide. His works, especially his shorter pieces, are immensely tuneful, with wonderful harmonies and belting key changes.

Recommended listening

Anthems 'A Gaelic Blessing' and 'For the Beauty of the Earth' (the latter a new twist on an old tune) are fine examples of the sumptuous Rutter harmonies.

WHITACRE, ERIC (B.1970)

Hearing Eric Whitacre's music for the first time can come as a surprise – an extremely pleasant surprise, for the dense texture of his music and the dissonances are a challenge to listen to. It's instantly a modern sound, and yet is hugely resonant of plainsong – it's absolutely lovely.

Eric Whitacre was born in America and lives in Britain. He was composer-in-residence at Sidney Sussex College, Cambridge, and he has his own UK-based professional choir.

He's well known for his 'virtual' choir, which he established in 2010. The most well-known piece performed by this virtual choir was his composition 'Lux Aurumque' ('Light and Gold'), sung by 185 choristers from all over the world. The singers recorded and uploaded their musical parts on video, and each video was then synchronised and combined into a single performance to create the virtual choir – Whitacre conducting the participants on a bank of computer screens.

His work as a composer, conductor and teacher is in huge demand worldwide – and all because he sang in Mozart's Requiem as an 18-year-old student; a life-changing moment for the young man who'd only ever dabbled in local rock bands up until then.

Recommended listening

His choral compositions 'Water Night' and 'Alleluia' are examples of his richly textured harmonies. His 'The Seal Lullaby' is a soft and mesmerising work.

PERFORMANCE ART

This genre can be scripted or unscripted, and the artist himself can use his body as the instrument, or he can use his fellow artistes or the audience, his actions interpreted as the 'art' of the performance.

THE ARTY ARTISTES

KLEIN, YVES (1928–62)

A 20-minute chord and then silence... well, 20 minutes of it. That is the essence of the Monotone-Silence Symphony, the work of French artist and performance artist Yves Klein, who died in 1962, aged 34. He stated that the symphony 'consisted of one unique continuous "sound" drawn out and deprived of its beginning and of its end, creating a feeling of vertigo and aspiration outside of time'. The only documented performance during his lifetime was at an art gallery in Paris, where Klein was conducting, accompanied by a group of naked models rolling themselves in blue paint, serving as 'living paint brushes'.

Similarly, La Monte Thornton Young's 'Dorian Blues in G' is a piece based on just one chord, shifting in and out of dissonance, and lasts 20 minutes.

THORNTON YOUNG, LA MONTE (B.1935)

From America comes artist, saxophonist and composer La Monte Thornton Young, who is regarded as the 'grandfather of minimalist music'. *Compositions 1960* is a set of performance art pieces, including three pieces for the American pianist David Tudor. Each piece has a set of instructions that the performer follows. The first instructions ask the performer to 'feed' the piano with a bale of hay and a bucket of water. The performer can 'feed' the piano, should they wish, or leave the piano to feed itself.

REICH, STEVE (B.1936)

Steve Reich, another minimalist composer, uses patterns, repeating themes and loops of melody to create what are strangely haunting pieces. His Piano Phase, for example, is performed by two pianists playing a rapidly repeating 12-note melody, the first keeping strict time, the other varying the tempo, until one 'catches up' with the other. A couple of musicians have played it solo, one hand on each of two pianos at 45-degree angles.

If you've never listened to his music, try 'Six Marimbas' and 'Clapping Music' for a start. First impressions can be that his music is too repetitive, but keep going, as there are hidden rhythms and syncopation that make his music hypnotic and rather soothing.

STOCKHAUSEN, KARLHEINZ (1928-2007)

German composer Karlheinz Stockhausen wrote 'Helicopter String Quartet' as the result of a dream, and it was first performed in 1995. The piece involves each of the four members of the quartet playing in four separate helicopters, so the technical problems getting them airborne, and being able to play in tune and together, were enormous.

LIGETI, GYÖRGY (1923-2006)

1. Take ten performers, and give each performer ten metronomes each.

2. Wind them all up, and set them all at different speeds.

3. Enter the conductor. Silence: how long for? Up to the conductor.

4. At the conductor's downbeat, the performers set the metronomes beating.

5. The performers leave the stage.

6. The metronomes wind down and as they stop, one by one, the remaining beats become clearer. Silence.

7. The performers then return to the stage.

You have just listened to the Hungarian composer György Ligeti's 'Poème Symphonique', composed in 1962. It is rarely heard but it is an hypnotic work, particularly when you get down to the last metronome slowly, slowly winding down...

CAGE, JOHN (1912-92)

Composer John Cage was an avant-garde composer who died in 1992. His early compositions owed much to the influence of Arnold Schoenberg and his 12-tone technique (see Glossary), but in later years he began to experiment and push the musical boundaries, devising innovative techniques with the tape recorder and the radio, and making modifications to the piano. He put forward the idea that the audience, merely by sitting there, can make its own music. 'There is no such thing as silence,' said Cage.

To this end, he composed the silent piece '4'33"', scored for any instrument, in order to explain to the audience that silence has its own musical notation. The performer enters the stage, the score instructing the performer not to play for the duration. The audience then listens to the sound that they and their surroundings make during the performance.

Another of John Cage's pieces which has to do with time is his 'Organ As SLow aS Possible (ASLSP)'. Originally a 20-minute piano piece, he adapted it for the organ in 1987 but didn't put in any instructions as to how slowly it should be performed, or how long it should take.

One performance (with a specially adapted organ) at Saint Burchardi Church in Halberstadt, Germany, began in 2001 and is scheduled to take 639 years to perform, ending in 2640. The piece began with two years of silence before the first chord was played, which sounded for two years; subsequent note changes were then every year or so, and the next one is scheduled for 5 September 2020. The project, begun by a group of philosophers and musicians, was created to challenge our concepts of time. Quite.

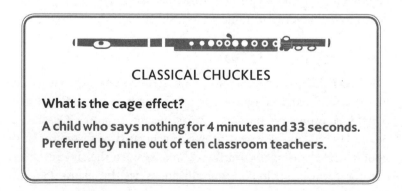

CLASSICAL CHUCKLES

What is the cage effect?

A child who says nothing for 4 minutes and 33 seconds. Preferred by nine out of ten classroom teachers.

GLOSSARY OF MUSICAL TERMS

A cappella
Italian for 'in the church style', meaning to sing without accompaniment.

Accidental
A symbol used to lower or raise the pitch of a note; a note that is not part of the key that is being played.

Arpeggio
A type of broken chord that is several notes of a chord played one after the other in quick succession.

Bar
A section on a musical stave to divide a composition into parts of equal time value.

Baritone
A male voice midway between tenor and bass.

Baton
The stick some conductors use to beat time. Not all conductors use one.

Bass
The lowest adult male voice.

Cadence
The fall of a melody phrase to its final note, in a sequence of chords.

Cantata
A short vocal work, sacred or secular, for single voices or a choir with an instrumental accompaniment.

Chamber music
Music played by a small orchestra in domestic surroundings or smaller concert halls.

Chord
The sounding together of three or more notes.

Chromatic
A music scale with all 12 half notes played (a semitone apart).

Clef
A sign placed at the beginning of a piece of music to denote the pitch of the notes. 'Clef' comes from the French word 'key'.

Coda
A musical 'tail' – the last part of a piece in addition to the usual form.

Concerto
A composition in three movements, with a solo instrument accompanied by an orchestra.

Contralto (also alto)
The lowest range of the female singing voice.

Counterpoint
Combining two or more independent melodic lines.

Diatonic
The seven-note major or minor scale.

Dissonance
The sounding of notes together which produces a harsh, discordant sound.

Divertimento
Italian for 'to amuse'. A musical genre describing a light hearted piece played at a social gathering, for example by a chamber ensemble.

Double-stopping
Playing two notes at once on a stringed instrument.

Finale
The last movement of a composition.

Fugue
A contrapuntal piece in two or more parts, introduced successively in imitation and repeated during the course of the music.

Glissando
A rapid sliding from one pitch to another over the keys of a piano or between the notes of the same string on a violin.

Harmony
Using notes simultaneously to produce chords, and chord progressions.

Harpsichord
A keyboard instrument shaped like a small grand piano, whose strings are plucked.

Kapellmeister
Kappelle – choir; *meister* – master.

Key
The tonality of a piece of music which is based on a particular major or minor scale.

Libretto
The text of an opera, or similar.

Lieder
Songs of the German Romantic period.

Melody
A succession of notes defined by pitch and rhythm.

Mezzo-soprano
The middle range female voice – between soprano and alto.

Minimalist music (attributed to the twentieth century)
'Simple' music with a contrapuntal edge, lots of broken chords, sliding harmonies and repetitions of beats and rhythms.

Movement
A complete section of a work such as a concerto or a symphony.

Octave
An interval of eight notes of the scale.

Opera
A classical musical work for the stage.

Op. (Opus)
The 'work' number assigned to a composition.

Oratorio
A vocal composition for soloists and choir, generally set to a sacred work.

Overture
An introductory piece of music to a major work, for example an opera.

Partita
An instrumental piece made up of a series of variations.

Perfect pitch
The ability to sing any note that is asked for by name, without having it played on an instrument.

Pizzicato
Instrument strings plucked with the finger, not the bow.

Prelude
A short instrumental or orchestral piece (can be similar to an overture) or a piece preceding a fugue.

Programme notes
A short history of the composers and descriptions of the pieces of music to be played in a concert, as a help to the audience.

Rondo
A piece with a main theme which recurs several times, alternating with contrasting sections or 'episodes'.

Scherzo
A lively, playful musical passage, performed in this way.

Sonata
A work in three or four movements, the first movement in sonata form.

Sonata form
Two musical themes which are set out, developed and reinstated.

Soprano
The highest female voice.

Symphony
An extended musical composition for an orchestra, usually in four movements.

Syncopation
The displacement of the musical accent to the offbeat.

Tenor
The highest male voice produced naturally, midway between baritone and alto.

Transposition
The process of turning a piece of music from one key to another.

12-tone technique
A musical technique created by Arnold Schoenberg, whereby all 12 notes of the scale are used in an order of tone relationship, one to another.

Vibrato
A regular, fluctuating, pulsating change of pitch.

FOREWORD BY
PIPPA GREENWOOD

FOR THE LOVE OF
RADIO 4

AN UNOFFICIAL
COMPANION

CAROLINE HODGSON

FOR THE LOVE OF RADIO 4

Caroline Hodgson

ISBN: 978-1-84953-642-4

Hardback

£9.99

From *Farming Today* at sunrise to the gentle strains of 'Sailing By' and the Shipping Forecast long after midnight, Radio 4 provides the soundtrack to life for millions of Britons. In *For the Love of Radio 4*, Caroline Hodgson celebrates all that's best about the nation's favourite spoken-word station, taking us on a tour through its history, its key personalities and programmes, and countless memorable moments from the archives.

'I found the book to be full of fascinating detail. It is clearly a labour of love, perfectly designed for Radio 4 lovers'

Simon Brett

'If you love Radio 4 it's impossible to turn it off. If you read this book it's impossible to put down'

Charles Collingwood

If you're interested in finding out more about our books, find us on Facebook at **Summersdale Publishers** and follow us on Twitter at **@Summersdale**.

www.summersdale.com

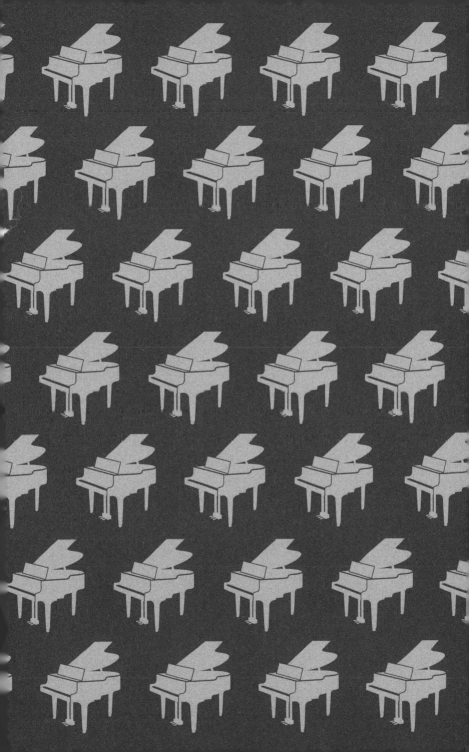

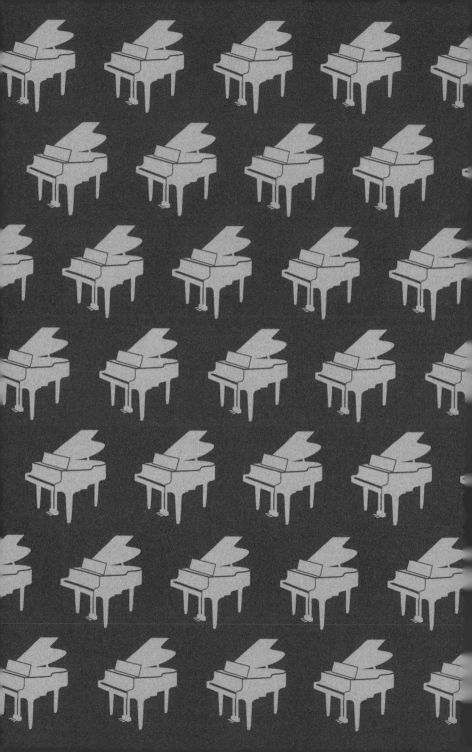